D1734173

An All-Consuming Passion for Jesus

Appeals to the Rising Generation

John Piper

Published by Desiring God
Post Office Box 2901
Minneapolis, MN 55402
www.desiringGod.org

Cover design and typesetting
Taylor Design Works

TABLE OF CONTENTS

INTRODUCTION

Friday morning, January 11, 2013 dawned frigid and dark in Minneapolis. John Piper finished his devotions, slid on his boots, bundled in his coat, and stepped outside to the remnants of an overnight ice storm to walk 600 slippery steps from his Minneapolis home to the door of Bethlehem Baptist Church for the weekly prayer gathering. The gatherings were typically small, sometimes only three or four attended, but two or three is enough of an audience to pray for the congregation's needs and the gospel's advance.

Just one week earlier, Piper took a different walk. Under the warm spotlight of Atlanta's Georgia Dome for Passion 2013, Piper climbed the stairs and walked on stage to plead with 60,000 college students to embrace the beauty of Christ as they face a future of inevitable suffering and persecution in various forms. His bold voice echoed through the dome, reiterating the point of the conference. "This is what Passion is about," he said, "the glorification of the infinite worth of Jesus so that he remains our joy when everything around our soul gives way" (Heb. 10:34). It was more than a message, it was a sobered theme of the conference, a theme of all the Passion Conferences.

With Piper again slated to preach at Passion 2014 in Atlanta, he has preached at every major Passion conference since 1997. With annual waves of new students, the Passion Conference crowd is never the same, but Piper's messages build on one another. And to get a sense of this development, we created this book to collect four of his pivotal messages from the conference, including his first Passion message, a two-part message: "Passion for the Supremacy of God" (1997), his message to 40,000 students: "Boasting Only in the Cross" (2000), along with "Getting to the Bottom of Your Joy" (2011), and his message to 60,000 students last year: "Joy as the Power to Suffer in the Path of Love for the Sake of Liberation" (2013).

But first I asked Pastor John to explain his history with Passion and what makes him so eager to speak at Louie Giglio's conferences, questions he was eager to answer on that icy January day in 2013 after he returned home from the prayer meeting. Here's what he said.

* * *

I have been to all the major American events since 1997, and I see Passion not just as an event but as a kind of movement that has lasted and grown. And it all grows out of Isaiah 26:8 which is where they get the "268 Generation" which says, "your name and your *renown* are the *desire* of our hearts" (NIV). Louie Giglio oversees Passion, and those two things, the *renown* of Christ and the *desire* of the soul, is what binds Louie and me together.

Louie came to my house in 1997 and we sat down at my

dining room table. We did not know each other, and he had heard and read some things. And he said, "I am looking for a person whose whole message revolves around the glory of God in Christ and you seem to me to be one of those." And we talked about Christian Hedonism and the relationship between *desiring* God on the one hand and God being glorified on the other hand. If you go to their app and look under "Who we are," they have almost word for word: "God is most glorified in us when we are most satisfied in Him."

That's what unites Louie and me. That's what the movement is. The movement is not about any particular cause, it is about the fame of Jesus. Louie stood up on the last day of Passion 2013 and said, "You would have to be blind not to know that what this is about is *Jesus* and the *fame of Jesus Christ*." You listen to their music and you watch Louie speak—this is about calling every new student generation to rivet their heart's affection and their mind's attention on the glory of Jesus Christ, the greatness and grandeur and wisdom and strength and power and blessing of Jesus Christ.

So that is what keeps my heart beating with Passion. They have focused in the last couple of years now on human trafficking, to try to put "feet" on our passion for Jesus by saying, "In Jesus' name and for Jesus' sake, we would love to see human slavery ended." And I think that is a beautiful, beautiful cause. (Find more information at enditmovement.com).

One of the reasons I love going back to Passion and being a part of it is that it embodies something I gave in my 2013 sermon. I want so bad to help cultivate in American

Evangelicalism a tone that is not chipper or glib or playful. And in my seventeen years at Passion, I have never heard a joke from the stage. I have never seen a silly skit from the stage. And that's remarkable when you think about it because a lot of student leaders think you have got to yuck it up with college students and be as silly as the latest comedian or the latest talk show host in order to make them feel like you are real. And Louie is not like that, and neither is Passion. And 60,000 students are coming for a blood-earnest singing and preaching event that exalts Jesus Christ. So, I just want to encourage leaders of students that it is possible to take this vision of that "sorrowful, yet always rejoicing" tone and build it into a student ministry (2 Cor. 6:10).

* * *

In the remainder of this book we offer four pivotal messages from Piper's eighteen-year involvement in the Passion conference. Taken together, these selected messages have been slightly edited and together offer a survey of the major themes of John Piper's ministry, fill out the concept of Christian Hedonism (and address from Scripture the most common objections to it).

Tony Reinke
Editor

PASSION FOR THE SUPREMACY OF GOD

[This chapter is a lightly edited transcript of two messages preached on January 2 and 3, 1997, at Passion97 in Austin, Texas. Audio is available online at http://dsr.gd/ passion1997]

I want to begin by giving you some of the reasons I was so eager to be here at this Passion conference.

My Mission in Life

One of the great advantages of being a pastor in one local church for many years is that over time the vision of the church and the vision of the pastor increasingly become one. A year ago our church produced a vision statement that goes like this: *We exist to spread a passion for the supremacy of God in all things for the joy of all peoples.* I can say without any hesitation that this is my life mission as well as the mission of our church.

So when I received the invitation, read about this conference, and saw the word "passion," and behind it the text of Isaiah 26:8—"your name and your renown is the desire of our hearts" (NIV)—I was hooked. I want to spread a passion for the supremacy of God in all things for the joy of all of you and all the peoples of this world. So that is reason number one why I'm here.

Glory to God

Reason number two is that I want to be a little match set to the kindling of your joy. I want you to leave from this place thrilled and happy in God.

And the third reason is I want you to see from Scripture that both reason one and reason two are the same reason. They are one. That is, to spread a passion for the supremacy of God and to be happy in God are the same pursuit. Because *God is most glorified in you when you are most satisfied in him*—which is the sentence that I'll come back to again and again.

The songs that we've been singing and the thirst we've been expressing are ways of giving glory to God. Because the more we find our satisfaction in him, the more we drink deeply from him and eat at the banquet table— which he is—the more his worth and his all-sufficiency are magnified. This is the angle on the gospel that God showed me in '68, '69, and '70 as he was doing a work in my life. There is no competition between God's passion to be glorified and our passion to be satisfied, because they are one.

Torching the Glacier

Here's another way to say this third reason for why I'm at Passion: *I'm here to torch a glacier.* I have a picture in my mind that comes from Matthew 24. In Matthew 24:12, while looking at the end of the age, Jesus says, "Lawlessness will be multiplied and the love of many will grow cold." I'm scared to death of growing cold. I hate the thought that my love for God, or my love for people, would one day freeze over. Yet Jesus says "It's coming!" It's coming like a glacier across the world. So part of my expectation for the last days is that lawlessness will be multiplied and that the love of many will grow cold. Now that could be a very bleak description of the last days.

But if you keep reading in Matthew 24, verse 13 says, "But those who endure to the end will be saved"—so somebody is going to endure. And the next verse (14) says, "And this gospel of the kingdom"—the good news about King Jesus who we're spreading a passion for—"this gospel of the kingdom *will* be preached as a testimony to all the nations, and then the end will come."

Now put verse 12 alongside verse 14. "Lawlessness will be multiplied and the love of many will grow cold," but "this gospel of the kingdom"—of Christ's sovereign, saving rule—"will spread to all the nations and then the end will come." There is a tension between these two verses. The tension is that it will not be cold people who are going to take the gospel back to their campuses. It's not cold people who are going to get the gospel to the unreached peoples of the world. How do I know that?

Let's back up a couple of verses, to verse nine, where

we find a prophetic word that is very different. Jesus says, "They will deliver you up to tribulation and put you to death. You will be hated by all nations on my account." Now if that's true—if we will be delivered up to the authorities in our missionary labor, if we will be killed, if we will be hated by every nation to which we will go—we know one thing that's clear: it isn't cold people who are delivering that message. It's white-hot worshipers of King Jesus who will get that done.

Therefore, what I see in verses 9–14 of Matthew 24 is that, as the end of the age draws near, there are going to be people who are getting ice cold and there are going to be people who are white-hot enough to lay down their lives for Jesus among all the peoples of the world.

So my ministry at my church, and my arrival here, is to torch a glacier.

I gave this image one time in my church and a little girl, about seven years old, came up to me after the service— I encourage the children in my church to draw my sermons—and she said, "Here's what I saw." She had drawn a marvelous glacier with Minneapolis written on it. It also had a little stick man holding up a torch, and there was a hole in the glacier, at the top. Over it was a lot of sunshine, coming down through the hole.

Now here is my eschatology in a nutshell: If you wonder what your campus is going to look like when Jesus comes, or what Austin, or Minneapolis, or wherever you're from, is going to look like, here it is: the glacier is moving, and a lot of people are growing cold towards God, but there is nothing in the Bible about the end times that says Bethlehem Baptist Church, or even "Minneapolis," or the

University of Texas at Austin, has to be under that glacier. Nothing! If there are enough people with torches lit white-hot for God, torching the glacier, a big hole can be opened up over your campus, over your local church, and even over your city. And that's why I'm here: I want to lift my torch.

Charles Spurgeon, a famous preacher in London over a hundred years ago, would say, "People come to watch me burn." They came to take their flickering little torch and stick it in his torch and go out and burn for Jesus another week. I would be thrilled if you brought a flickering torch here today and put it in my fire. That's why I'm here.

Foundation First, Then Application

There is a foundation for what I want to do. My task first is to talk about living for the glory of God, having a passion for the glory of God. I have two parts in mind here. First is foundation, and second is application.

The foundation is this: Your passion for the supremacy of God in all things is based squarely on God's passion for the supremacy of God in all things. Your God-centeredness—if it's going to endure—has to be rooted in God's God-centeredness. If you want God to be supreme in your life, you have to see, and believe, and love the truth that God is supreme in the life of God. If you want God to be your treasure—as we've sung about here at Passion— so that you value God more than anything, you have to see and believe that God's greatest treasure is God, that he treasures himself more than he treasures anything. We may not withhold from God the highest pleasure in the universe, namely, the worship of God. That's foundation; that's what I want to address in part one.

And then in part two, I want to talk about your pursuit of joy in God, and that this pursuit is necessarily implied in God's pursuit of his glory in your life.

* * *

Part One:

God's Passion for His Glory

Let me begin with a little story. I spoke at my *alma mater*, Wheaton College, several years ago. It was my first chance to speak in the big, blue, beautiful, chandeliered chapel. I stood up and said, "The chief end of God is to glorify God and enjoy him forever." And all my friends who were up in the balcony thought, "Oh no, he blew it on his first chance at his own *alma mater* to speak to these students. He comes back after 20 years, and he misquotes the Westminster Catechism right off the bat saying, 'The chief end of God' instead of 'The chief end of man.'" And to their great relief, I went on to say that I really meant what I said. I hadn't misspoken. And I really mean it now: *the chief end of God is to glorify God and enjoy himself forever.*

I grew up in the home of an evangelist. My dad, Bill Piper, taught me from an early age 1 Corinthians 10:31: "Whatever you do, whether you eat or whether you drink, do everything to the glory of God." But I never heard anybody say that God does everything to the glory of God. And that the root of my living for the glory of God is that God lives for the glory of God.

I had never seen a child bring home a Sunday School paper that said, "God loves himself more than he loves you, and therein lies the only hope that he might love you, unworthy as you are." Most of us grew up in homes, and in churches, where we got excited about being Christians to the degree that we thought God was excited about us, not to the degree that we got excited about a God-centered God.

It's very easy in a man-centered world, where self-esteem is the highest value, to be a Christian to the degree that it buttresses what you would've done anyway, without God. Who wouldn't be a Christian? Well, you're not truly a born-again Christian if you only love what you would've loved without being confronted with the beauty of a God-centered God. If God is only a means to your self-advancement and exaltation—rather than your seeing in him something infinitely glorious, as a God consumed with the manifestation of his glory—then you need to check your conversion. So this is a big reality check. Very few people have ever said to me, or shown me what I've now seen in the Bible, that God chose me for his glory.

Saved for Glory

I remember teaching a class on Ephesians 1 in January of 1976 in what we called "Interim" at Bethel College in those days, and working my way systematically through the first fourteen verses of Ephesians and having my mind boggled again. Because three times—in verses 6, 12, and 14—Paul says that God chose us in Jesus before the foundation of the world and he predestined us to be his sons *to the praise of the glory of his grace.*

He chose you. Why? That his glory and grace might be praised and magnified. Your salvation is to glorify God. Your election is to glorify God. Your regeneration is to glorify God. Your justification is for the glory of God. Your sanctification is for the glory of God. And one day your glorification will be an absorbance into the glory of God.

You were created for the glory of God. Isaiah 43:6–7: "Bring my sons from afar, and my daughters from the ends of the earth; everyone whom I created *for my glory*."

God rescued his people Israel from Egypt for his glory. Psalm 106:7–8: "Our fathers, when they were in Egypt, did not consider your ways or your wonderful works. They rebelled against you at the Red Sea. Yet you saved them *for your name's sake*, that you might make known your power and your glory."

In other words, he split the Red Sea and saved his rebellious people, so that he might make known his mighty power. And it spread all the way to Jericho and saved a prostitute, so that when the Israelites came there and were ready to blow the trumpets, she had already been born again, because she said, "We heard your name and your renown." And one woman and her family believed in a God-centered God and escaped destruction.

God had mercy on Israel in the wilderness for his glory. God spared Israel in the wilderness over and over again. "The house of Israel rebelled against me in the wilderness," Ezekiel says, quoting God, "and I thought I would pour out my wrath, but I acted for the sake of my name lest it be profaned among the nations" (20:13–14). And then finally God sends them into judgment in Babylon, and after 70 years, mercy warms to them. He will not divorce his covenant bride, and he brings them back. But why?

What's the motive rooted in God's heart? Listen to it from Isaiah 48:9–11: "*For my name's sake* I defer my anger, *for the sake of my praise* I restrain it for you, that I may not cut you off. Behold, I have refined you, but not like silver; I have tried you in the furnace of affliction. *For my own sake, for my own sake*, I do it, for how should *my name* be profaned? *My glory* I will not give to another." That's a God-centered motive for mercy.

Jesus came and died for God's glory. Jesus came into the world for what reason? Oh, how many times we have quoted John 3:16. And it is gloriously true. And before this message is finished, I hope you'll see that this emphasis (God's glory) and the emphasis you've known for a long time (your joy) are not at odds.

But why did Jesus come? According to Romans 15:8–9, he came for this reason: "Christ became a servant to the circumcision to show God's truthfulness, in order to confirm the promises given to the patriarchs, and in order that the Gentiles might *glorify God* for his mercy." Jesus came to earth, became fully human, and died so that you would give glory to his Father for mercy. He came for his Father's sake. That's the main reason why he came, for his Father's glory. And his glory reaches its apex in the overflow of mercy.

Listen to this word from Romans 3:25–26: "God put Christ forward as a propitiation by his blood to demonstrate God's righteousness. It was to prove at the present time that he himself is righteous." That's why he died. He died to vindicate the righteousness of God who had passed over sins like David's adultery and murder.

Did it ever trouble you that God just passed over King

David's adultery, and David just went on being king? Well, it troubled Paul to the depths of his being that God is not righteous to pass over sins. And it wasn't just David. There were thousands of saints in the Old Testament, and today, whose sins God simply forgets and passes over. And Paul cried out, "How can you be God and do that? How can you be righteous and do that? How can you be just and do that? How can you be worthy of worship and do that?" If any judge in Austin did that—if he acquitted a guilty child-abuser, a rapist, or a murderer—he'd be off the bench in a minute. And yet God does it every day, so we might ask, "What kind of God are you?"

The cross is the solution to a mega-theological problem, namely, *How can God be God and forgive sins*? Jesus came to vindicate God in the saving of people like you and me. Salvation is a grandly and gloriously God-centered thing.

Jesus is returning to get glory. Why is he coming again? Jesus is coming, and let me tell you why he is coming and what you can do when he comes, so that you'll be ready and do it. 2 Thessalonians 1:8–10: "Those who do not obey the gospel will suffer the punishment of eternal destruction and exclusion from the presence of the Lord and from the glory of his might, when *he comes on that day to be glorified in his saints and to be marveled at in all who have believed.*" You see those two things? He is coming to be glorified (magnified) in his saints, and to be marveled at. If you don't get started on that now, you won't be able to do it when he comes.

This conference exists to light a fire in your bones, and to ignite a fire in your minds, and to ignite a fire in your hearts to get you ready to meet King Jesus so that you can continue throughout all eternity doing what he created you to do; namely, to marvel at him and magnify him.

Magnify God Like a Telescope

So magnify Jesus by marveling at him, but don't magnify him like a microscope. You know the difference between two kinds of magnification, don't you? There's *telescope* magnification and *microscope* magnification, and it's blasphemy to magnify God like a microscope.

To magnify God like a microscope is to take something tiny and make it look bigger than it is. If you try to do that to God, you blaspheme. But a telescope puts its lens on unimaginable expanses of greatness and tries simply to help them look more like what they are. That's what a telescope is for.

Twinkle, twinkle, little star—we look up in the sky at night, and they look like mere pin-points. But as you know, that's not what they are. They are big. Really, really big. And they are hot! And we wouldn't have much of a clue about that except that once upon a time somebody invented telescopes. And astronomers put their eyes to them and did calculations and thought, "It's bigger than the earth, millions of times bigger than the earth."

That's the way God is. Your life exists to telescope God's glory to your campus. That's a big calling. That's where we're headed in Part Two.

If God Is God-Centered, How Can He Be Loving?

Here's the key question to end Part One, because I can feel an objection rising at this point. For twenty years I've been teaching this truth that God is a God-centered God and that his God-centeredness is the root of my God-centeredness, and at this point the question begins to rise: "This does not sound loving, because the Bible says in 1 Corinthians 13:5, 'Love seeks not its own.' And you're telling us now that God spends *all* of his time seeking his own. So either God is not loving, or you're a liar." And that's a big problem. So let me try to answer how it is that God is loving in seeking his own self-exaltation.

Help from C.S. Lewis

I found the key in C.S. Lewis. If any of you have read my book *Desiring God* then you remember this quote. Lewis was a pagan until his late twenties, and he hated what he thought was God's vanity. He said that every time he read the words in the Psalms, "Praise the Lord, Praise the Lord"—and he knew Christian doctrine, that the Psalms were God-inspired—he knew that it was really God saying, "Praise me, Praise me" and it sounded like, he thought, "an old woman seeking compliments." That's a quote from Lewis's *Reflections on the Psalms*. And then suddenly God came into Lewis's life. And this is what he wrote:

> The most obvious fact about praise, whether of God or anything, strangely escaped me. I thought of it in terms of compliment, approval, giving of honor. I had never noticed that all enjoyment spontaneously overflows in praise, unless sometimes we bring shyness in to check it. The world rings with praise: lovers praising their mistresses, readers their favorite poets, walkers

praising the countryside, players praising their favorite games, praise of weather, wines, dishes, actors, horses, colleges, countries, historical personages, children, flowers, mountains, rare stamps, rare beetles, even sometimes politicians and scholars. My whole more general difficulty with the praise of God depended on my absurdly denying to us, as regards the supremely valuable, what we delight to do—even what we cannot help doing—with regard to everything else we value.

And then here comes the key sentences:

> I think we delight to praise what we enjoy because the joy is not complete until it is expressed. It is not out of compliment that lovers keep on telling one another how beautiful they are. The delight is incomplete until it is expressed.

That was the key for me that unlocked how God can be both loving and self-exalting in everything he does. Let me put the pieces together for you.

The Answer to the Question

If God is to love you, what must he give you? He must give you what is best for you. And the best thing in all the universe is God. If he were to give you all health, the best job, the best spouse, the best computer, the best vacations, and the best success in any realm, and yet withhold himself, then he would amount in the end to hating you. But if he gives you himself, even if nothing besides, he loves you infinitely.

We must have God for our enjoyment if God is to be

loving to us. Now Lewis has said that if God gives you himself to enjoy for all eternity, that joy will not come to consummation until you express it in praise. Therefore, for God to love you fully, he cannot be indifferent to whether you bring your joy to consummation through praise or not. Therefore, God must seek our praise if we are to be loved by him.

Let me run that by you one more time. That's the essence of my life message. And I believe it's at the heart of the Bible: To love you, God must give you what is best for you. *God is what is best for you.* "In your presence is fullness of joy; at your right hand are pleasures evermore" (Ps. 16:11). God gives himself to us for our pleasure. But Lewis has shown us that unless those pleasures find expression in praise to God, the pleasures are restricted. And therefore, God, not wanting to restrict your pleasure in any way, says, "Praise me. In everything you do, praise me. In everything you do, exalt me. In everything you do, have a passion for my supremacy"—which simply means that God's passion to be glorified and your passion to be satisfied are not at odds. They come together. *God is most glorified in you when you are most satisfied in him.*

Now that's the end of Part One. Let me tell you where we're going in Part Two. If this is true, that God is most glorified in you when you are most satisfied in him—and therefore, there is no tension or contradiction between your satisfaction in him and his glorification in you—then the vocation of your life is to pursue your pleasure. I call it *Christian Hedonism*, and I want to talk about how you do that and why it will transform your relationships, your campuses, your worship, and your eternity.

Part Two:

Our Passion for God's Glory

Part One was an attempt to torch the glacier and to spread a passion for the supremacy of God in all things for the joy of all peoples. I hope I've sufficiently made the point that God does everything he does for the glory of his name. God magnifies God. The most passionate heart in all the universe for God is God's heart. That's the main point. This Passion conference is about God's passion for God. Everything he does, from creation to consummation, he does with a view to displaying and upholding the glory of his name.

God's God-Centeredness Is Not Unloving

The second point from Part One was that this is not unloving. The reason it is not unloving for God to exalt himself in this way is because knowing God, and being swept up into the praises of God, is what satisfies the human soul. We saw in Psalm 16:11 that in God's presence is fullness of joy, and at his right hand are pleasures forevermore. Therefore, if God's exalting himself—to the degree that we can see him for who he is—satisfies our souls, then God is the one being in all the universe for whom self-exaltation is the highest virtue and the essence of love.

We creatures may not copy the Creator in this. To the degree that we exalt ourselves for another person to enjoy, we are hateful, not loving, because we distract them from the one being who really can satisfy their souls. Therefore, we may not imitate God in his God-ness. God is the one and only absolutely unique being in all the universe for whom self-exaltation is the essence and the foundation of love. It has to be this way if he is God.

We might want him to love like humans love, by making others central, but he can't do that and still be God. He is infinitely valuable in himself. There is none besides God. Therefore, to put it bluntly, he is "stuck" with being magnificent and glorious and all-sufficient and self-sufficient, without any need of us whatsoever. This is the foundation of grace. If you try to make yourself the center of grace, it ceases to be grace. God-centered grace is biblical grace.

My delight is not in God making me the center of the universe. My delight is in God being the center of the universe, forever, and drawing me up into his fellowship, to see him, know him, enjoy him, treasure him, be satisfied in him, for all the days of eternity.

The Implications of God's God-Centeredness for Mankind

Now we turn to Part Two. If what I have said so far is true, if it is biblical, then there is a stunning implication for your life. It is this: what you should do is make it your vocation to be as happy as you possibly can be *in God*. So my call to you in the rest of this message, in the name of God Almighty, is that you might make it your eternal vocation to pursue your pleasure with all the might that God mightily inspires within you.

My problem in life, and your problem in life, is not that we are pursuing our pleasure when we ought to be doing our duty. That is not God's or the Bible's assessment of our problem. Lewis had it exactly right in his life-changing sermon, "The Weight of Glory," when he said that our problem is that we are far too easily pleased, not that we are pursuing our pleasure too eagerly. He says that we are like children fooling around making mud pies in the slums because we cannot imagine what a vacation at the beach is like. Our problem is that we are clutching tin idols to ourselves when golden reality stands before us. We are far too easily pleased. The problem with the world is not hedonism; it's the failure of hedonism to pursue what is truly satisfying.

And the implication is that you should get up in the morning and say, like George Mueller said, before you go out and do anything, "I must have my heart happy in God or I will be of no use to anybody. I'll use them and try to get them to satisfy my cravings and my vacancies." If you want to be a person of love, if you want to be released to lay down your life for other people, you must make it your aim to be happy in God.

But we are far too easily pleased. We have settled for such small, short-lived, inadequate, non-satisfying pleasures that our capacities for joy have so shriveled up to the point that we have made joyless duty the essence of virtue so as to conceal our untransformed hearts that cannot be moved by God. How escapist is that? So I am on a campaign against the Stoics and Immanuel Kant, the philosopher of the Enlightenment who said that to the degree that you seek your benefit in any moral act, you diminish its virtue. That idea is not in the Bible. It destroys worship, virtue, courage, and God-centeredness everywhere. It elevates man, the virtuous one who does his duty without any view to God to satisfy his soul. Fie on it! May it be gone from our hearts forever!

I'm on a campaign against the sentiment that hangs in the evangelical air. I started on this campaign about 25 years ago, and I've been on it ever since, trying to raise my family in it, build a church on it, write books about it, trying to live it. Little by little, the objections come. That's the way you grow. Several of you have said to me that you feel like your world is being turned by this conference. Paradigms are being shaken. Copernican Revolutions are in the offing, and that's just the way you start changing. It may take 15 years and objection after objection.

In 1968, I started seeing some of these things with the help of one of my seminary professors, and then C.S. Lewis, and then Jonathan Edwards, and King David, and Saint Paul, and Jesus Christ. And the way that my mind works is that one objection after the other comes up and I cringe, and then I go to the Bible and I weep and cry and struggle and ask and pray and talk. Then little by little the objections refine the vision.

So here are five objections to what I've been saying.

Five Objections to Answer

1. Does the Bible really teach that you should pursue your joy with all your heart and mind and soul and strength, or is that just John Piper's clever way of getting attention?

2. What about self-denial? Didn't Jesus say, "If anyone would come after me, let him deny himself?"

3. Doesn't this put too much emphasis on emotion? Isn't Christianity essentially a matter of the will, whereby we make commitments and decisions?

4. What becomes of the noble concept of serving God as a duty when it's hard and you don't feel like it?

5. Doesn't this just put me—and not God—at the center of things?

1. Does the Bible Really Teach That You Should Pursue Your Joy?

My answer is yes, and it does so in at least four ways.

a) With commandments

Consider Psalm 37:4: "Delight yourself in the LORD." This is not a suggestion. This is a commandment. If you believe, "Thou shalt not commit adultery" is something you should obey, then you should also obey, "Delight yourself in the LORD."

Or Psalm 32:11: "Be glad in the LORD, and rejoice, O righteous ones, and shout for joy all you upright in heart." Or Psalm 100:2: "Serve the Lord with gladness."

That's a commandment: "Serve the LORD with gladness!" To the degree that you are indifferent to whether you serve the Lord with gladness or not, you are indifferent to God. He told you to serve him with gladness. Or Philippians 4:4: "Rejoice in the Lord always, and again I say, rejoice."

These commands to pursue joy are all over the Bible. We're talking commandments. That's the first way the Bible teaches this.

b) With threats

Jeremy Taylor once said, "God threatens terrible things if we will not be happy." I thought it was clever when I first heard it. But it's not just clever, it's a quotation from Deuteronomy 28:47–48, and it's devastating. "Because you did not serve the LORD your God with joyfulness and gladness of heart, therefore you shall serve your enemies whom the LORD will send against you." God threatens terrible things if we will not be happy in him. Is that not a warrant for hedonism? Is that not a warrant to making it your life vocation to pursue your joy in God with all your might?

c) By presenting saving faith as essentially being satisfied with all that God is for you in Jesus

For example, Hebrews 11:6: "Without faith it is impossible to please God, for he who would draw near to God must believe that he is and that he is a rewarder of those who seek him." If you would please God, you must have faith. What is faith? Coming to God precisely with the deep conviction that he is going to reward us for coming. If we don't believe that, or if we go to God for any other reason, we do not please God.

Or take John 6:35. Jesus says, "I am the bread of life. He who comes to me will never hunger, and he who believes in me will never thirst." The one who believes in Jesus will never thirst. What does that mean about faith? What is faith? Faith, in the apostle John's theology, is a coming to Jesus for the satisfaction of our souls such that nothing else can satisfy. That's faith. This is simply basic Christianity in a language many of us are less familiar.

d) By defining sin as the insanity of forsaking the pursuit of your pleasure in God

Sin is the insanity of forsaking the pursuit of your pleasure in God. Jeremiah 2:12–13: "Be appalled, O heavens, be shocked. Be utterly desolate, says the LORD. For my people have committed two great evils. They have forsaken me, the fountain of living waters, and have hewed out for themselves cisterns, broken cisterns that can hold no water."

Tell me, what is evil? What is the definition of evil, that which appalls the universe, that causes the angels of God to say, "No! It can't be!" According to Jeremiah 2:12–13, evil is looking at God, the fountain of all-satisfying, living water, and saying, "No, thank you," and turning to the television, sex, parties, booze, money, prestige, a house in the suburbs, a vacation, a new computer program, and saying, "Yes!" That's evil.

In those four ways, at least, the Bible confirms that what I'm saying here is true when I say *devote your life to the pursuit of your satisfaction in God*. So objection number one falls.

2. What About Self-Denial?

Didn't Jesus say in Mark 8:34, "Whoever would come after me, let him deny himself and take up his cross"? The cross is a place where you die. It's a place of execution. It's not a cranky mother-in-law, or a bad roommate, or a disease in your bones. It's death of the self. So then, am I heretical in calling you to pursue the satisfaction of your souls as a life-vocation? I've felt that objection—and then I read the next verse: "for he who would save his life will lose it, and he who loses his life for my sake will save it." What is Jesus's logic in these verses? The logic is this...

> "O my disciples, don't lose your life. Don't lose
> your life. Save your life! Save your life!"
> "How, Jesus?"
> "Lose it."
> "I don't get it. I don't get it, Jesus."
> "What I mean is—my disciples, my loved ones—
> lose your life in the sense that you lose everything
> but me. 'Unless a grain of wheat falls to the ground
> and dies, it remains alone. But if it dies, it bears
> much fruit' (Jn. 12:24). Die to the world. Die to
> prestige, die to wealth, die to illicit sex, die to
> cheating to get ahead, die to the need for people to
> approve you. Die, and have me."

I believe in self-denial. Deny yourself tin to have gold. Deny yourself sand to stand on a rock. Deny yourself brackish water to have wine. There is no ultimate self-denial—nor did Jesus ever mean it that way.

I believe in self-denial. I believe this word about Jesus from Jesus in Matthew 13:44. "The kingdom of heaven is like a man who found a treasure hidden in a field and, *in his joy*, he went and sold everything he had to buy that field." You call that self-denial? Yes! He sold everything. He counted everything as refuse and rubbish that he might gain Christ.

So, yes, it's self-denial—and no, it isn't ultimate self-denial. There is a self that should be crucified—the self that loves the world. But the new self—the self that loves

Christ above all things and finds its satisfaction in him—don't kill that self. That's the new creation. Glut that self on God.

O, I believe in self-denial. I believe in the self-denial that the rich young ruler couldn't understand, but that Jesus taught in that moment: "Go, sell everything you've got, young man, and come follow me, and you'll have treasure in heaven." And he wouldn't do it. And Jesus said to his disciples, "It is really hard for a rich man to get into the kingdom of heaven. It's easier for a camel to go through the eye of a needle than for rich people to get into the kingdom of heaven." Then the disciples were absolutely stunned, and they said, "Who then can be saved?" And Jesus said, "With men it is impossible. Nobody can have the heart I'm calling for on their own. But with God," he says, "all things are possible." And then Peter pipes up, "We left everything to follow you. What about us? We really sacrificed." And Jesus responds (I wish I knew the tone of his voice) and says, "Peter, no one has left houses or mother or father or brothers or sisters or lands or children for my sake who will not receive back one-hundred fold of mothers, sisters, brothers, lands, and children, in this life—along with persecutions—and in the age to come, eternal life. You cannot sacrifice anything that will not be repaid to you a thousand-fold. Don't pity yourself when your head gets chopped off for me" (see Mark 10:17–31).

Yes, I believe in self-denial. I believe in denying myself everything that would stand in the way of me being satisfied fully in God, and that's how I understand what the Bible means by self-denial. I believe that the great missionaries David Livingstone and Hudson Taylor, having come to the end of their lives and having lost wives and health and everything else except one thing, were absolutely right to say to Cambridge University students and people elsewhere, "I never made a sacrifice." I know what they mean, and you know what they mean. And I believe that Jim Elliot who laid down his life as a young man was absolutely right to say, "He is no fool who gives what he cannot keep to gain what he cannot lose." That's what I believe about self-denial. So objection number two falls.

3. Aren't You Making Too Much Out of Emotions?

Isn't Christianity essentially "decision"? Commitment of the will? Aren't emotions just tag-along, optional, icing on the cake? You may think that this way of talking about Christianity elevates emotions to an unbiblical place of prominence.

But then we read the Bible—it helps to read the Bible when you're in an argument—and we see that:

› We are commanded to feel joy: "Rejoice in the Lord" (Phil. 4:4).

› We are commanded to feel hope: "Hope in God" (Ps. 42:5).

› We are commanded to feel fear: "Fear him who can cast both soul and body into hell" (Luke 12:5).

› We are commanded to feel peace: "Let the peace of Christ rule in your hearts" (Col. 3:15).

› We are commanded to feel zeal: "Be aglow (literally 'boil') in the Spirit, never flag in zeal" (Rom. 12:11). This is not optional, this is not icing. It's a commandment! "Never flag in zeal."

› We are commanded to feel grief: "Weep with those who weep" (Rom. 12:15). You don't have an option. You've got to weep, you've got to feel weeping with those who weep.

› We are commanded to feel desire: "Earnestly desire the sincere spiritual milk of the word" (1 Pet. 2:2). It's not an option. You can't say, "Well, I can't turn desire on enough, so how can I obey this? It can't really be a command." Wrong! Yes, you cannot turn these feelings on and off at will. No, they are still obligations. Therein lies our desperate condition that we heard about in Part One.

Everything the Bible commands us to do in these passages above, we cannot do simply by willpower or decision or commitment. We can only do it by miracle. Aren't we desperate? Isn't it a desperate thing to be told by Almighty God that we must do what we cannot do? If our hearts were right, we would do them. But we are depraved, and we are commanded to feel tender-heartedness: "Be kind to one another, tender-hearted" (Eph. 4:32). We can't just say that forgiveness means saying, "I'm sorry." We must feel it.

We're commanded to feel gratitude. Take a child on Christmas morning who gets a present from grandma— and it's black socks! Yuck! And then his father says to him, "Say thank you to your grandmother." And then the kid says, "Thank you for the socks." That's not what the Bible is talking about. The kid can do that by willpower. But he cannot feel gratitude for those socks by willpower.

Neither can you feel gratitude to God by your willpower in accordance with the command in Ephesians 5:20 to "be thankful for everything." Well then, we're done for, unless Almighty God works.

So you can see, I don't buy objection number three. I don't believe that I'm elevating affections and feelings and emotions higher than the Bible does. I think I'm reinstating them to the place from where a decisionistic, commitment-laden, willpower-American, we-can-do-it religion dropped them because they're out of our control.

4. What About the Noble Vision of Serving God?

Isn't it a duty to serve God? Someone may say, "It doesn't sound like service in your way of talking about Christianity, Piper." It just doesn't sound the same as service—dutiful, rising to the challenge of performing the will of God when it's hard.

To which I have learned now to respond, "Let's look at a few texts that shape the metaphor of servanthood." All metaphors about your relationship to God, whether it's as a servant, or son or daughter, or friend, have elements in them which, if you stressed them, would be false. They also have elements in them which, if you stressed them, would be true. Now what is false and what is true in the analogy of servanthood?

The texts that help us separate the two so that we don't blaspheme when we serve are texts like Acts 17:25: "God is not served by human hands, as though he needed anything. But he himself gives to all men life and breath and everything." *God is not served.* Be careful. He is not served as though he needed you or your service. He doesn't.

Or take a text like Mark 10:45: "The Son of Man came not to be served but to give his life as a ransom for many." *He came not to be served.* Watch out! Watch out! If you undertake to serve him, then you cross his purpose! Perplexing though, isn't it? Paul called himself the servant of the Lord in every letter almost. And here in Acts 17:25 and Mark 10:45, it says that God is not served and that the Son of Man came not to be served. There must be a kind of service that is evil and a kind of service that is good. What is the good service?

The good service is 1 Peter 4:11: "Let him who serves serve in the strength that God supplies, that in everything God may get the glory." God is not served by human hands as though he needed anything. We must find a way to worship, type papers, listen to lectures, drive a car, change a diaper, and preach a sermon, and all in such a way that we are always the receiver. Because the giver gets the glory, and the receiver gets the joy. Anytime we cross Acts 17:25— "God is not served by humans hands [as though he were a receiver,] as though he needed anything"—we blaspheme.

Yesterday I gave an illustration to the leadership crew of this conference from Matthew 6:24 about service. "You cannot serve two masters. Either you'll hate the one and love the other. Or either you'll be devoted to one and despise the other. You cannot serve both God and money." So here we're talking service. How do you serve money? You do not serve money by meeting money's needs. You serve money by posturing your life relentlessly, with all of your energy and time and effort, to benefit from money. Your mind spins with how to make the shrewd investment, how to find the best deal, how to invest where it's low so that it'll go high, and you're consumed with how to benefit from money, because money is your source.

If that's true about the way you serve money, how then do you serve God? It's exactly the same. You posture yourself, and you maneuver your life, and you devote energy and effort and time and creativity to positioning yourself under the waterfall of God's continual blessing, so that he remains the source and you remain the empty receiver. You remain the beneficiary; he remains the benefactor. You remain hungry; he remains the bread. You remain thirsty; he remains the water. You don't ever do the blasphemous role-reversal on God.

We must find a way to serve that is in the strength that God supplies. If I am on the receiving end when I am serving, then I put God in the position of a beneficiary. I become his benefactor, and now I am God. And there are many such religions in the world. So objection four falls.

5. Aren't You Just Making Yourself Central?

"You talk about pursuing your joy and your pleasure," someone might say. "You talk about duty as something else than what we've always known, and you say that we must be careful about service. It sounds to me like you're maneuvering and manipulating biblical language just to make yourself central." That would be the most devastating criticism of all, wouldn't it?

Here's my answer: I've been married to my wife Noël since December 21, 1968. I love her a lot. We've been through a lot together, both really hard times and really good times. We've seen our teenage kids through some incredibly difficult teenage years. I cry most easily when I think about my sons and my little girl. Suppose on December 21 next year I come home with dozens of long-stem red roses behind my back (one for each year) and ring the doorbell. Noël comes to the door, looks sort of puzzled about why I would be ringing my own doorbell, and I pull the roses out and say, "Happy Anniversary, Noël!" And she says, "Johnny, they're beautiful! Why did you?" And I say, "It's my duty."

Wrong answer. Let's back it up and try it again.

[Ding-dong]
"Happy Anniversary, Noël!"
"Johnny, they're beautiful! Why did you?"
"Nothing makes me happier than to buy you roses. In fact, why don't you go change clothes, and we'll go do something special tonight, because there is nothing I would rather do than spend the evening with you."

Right answer.

Why? Why wouldn't she say, "You're the most selfish Christian Hedonist I've ever met! All you ever think about is what makes *you* happy!" What's going on here? Why is duty the wrong answer and delight the right answer?

If you get this, then you've got what I've been getting at in this message. My wife is most glorified in me when I am most satisfied in her. If I try to change our relationship into a service relationship, into a duty relationship, where I do not pursue my pleasure in her, she will be belittled. And so will God.

When you get to heaven and the Father looks at you and says, "Why are you here? Why did you lay down your life for me?" you better not say, "It was my duty to come, because I'm a Christian." You better say, "Where else would I want to go? To whom else could I turn? You are my soul's desire!"

And that is what this Passion conference is about. This conference is about two great things coming together in the 268 Generation from Isaiah 26:8. It is the passion of God for his name and renown, and the passion of my heart to be satisfied in all of my desires. Those are two unshakable things in the universe. And what I hope you have seen is that they are one, because God and his name and his renown are most glorified in me when I am most satisfied in him.

BOASTING ONLY IN THE CROSS

[This message was preached on May 20, 2000 at OneDay2000 in Shelby Farms, Tennessee, and it appears in chapter form in Don't Waste Your Life *(Crossway Books, 2003), pages 43–59. Thanks to Crossway for permission to reprint here. Audio of this message is available online at http://dsr.gd/passion2000 .]*

The opposite of wasting your life is living life by a single God-exalting, soul-satisfying passion. The well-lived life must be God-exalting and soul-satisfying because that is why God created us (Isa. 43:7; Ps. 90:14). And "passion" is the right word (or, if you prefer, zeal, fervor, ardor, blood-earnestness) because God commands us to love him with *all* our heart (Matt. 22:37), and Jesus reminds us that he spits lukewarm people out of his mouth (Rev. 3:16). The opposite of wasting your life is to live by a single, soul-satisfying passion for the supremacy of God in all things.

How serious is this word "single"? Can life really have that much "singleness" of purpose? Can work and leisure and relationships and eating and lovemaking and ministry all really flow from a single passion? Is there something deep enough and big enough and strong enough to hold all that together? Can sex and cars and work and war and changing diapers and doing taxes really have a God-exalting, soul-satisfying unity?

This question drives us to the death of Jesus on the cross. Living for the glory of God must mean living for the glory of Christ crucified. Christ is the image of God. He is the sum of God's glory in human form. And his beauty shines most brightly at his darkest hour.

Pressed by the Bible to Know One Thing

But we are driven to the same bloody place also by the question of a *single* passion. The Bible pushes us in this direction. For example, the apostle Paul said that his life and ministry were riveted on a single aim: "I decided to know nothing among you except Jesus Christ and him crucified" (1 Cor. 2:2). That is astonishing, when you think of all the varied things Paul did, in fact, talk about. There must be a sense in which "Jesus Christ and him crucified" is the ground and sum of everything else he says. He is pushing us to see our lives with a single focus, and for the cross of Christ to be that focus.

You don't have to know a lot of things for your life to make a lasting difference in the world. But you do have to know the few great things that matter, perhaps just one, and then be willing to live for them and die for them. The people that make a durable difference in the world are not the people who have mastered many things, but who have been mastered by one great thing. If you want your life to count, if you want the ripple effect of the pebbles you drop to become waves that reach the ends of the earth and roll on into eternity, you don't need to have a high IQ. You don't have to have good looks or riches or come from a fine family or a fine school. Instead you have to know a few great, majestic, unchanging, obvious, simple, glorious things—or one great all-embracing thing—and be set on fire by them.

A Tragedy in the Making

You may not be sure that you want your life to make a difference. Maybe you don't care very much whether you make a lasting difference for the sake of something great. You just want people to like you. If people would just like being around you, you'd be satisfied. Or if you could just have a good job with a good wife, or husband, and a couple of good kids and a nice car and long weekends and a few good friends, a fun retirement, and a quick and easy death, and no hell—if you could have all that (even without God)—you would be satisfied. That is a tragedy in the making. A wasted life.

These Lives and Deaths Were No Tragedy

In April 2000, Ruby Eliason and Laura Edwards were killed in Cameroon, West Africa. Ruby was over eighty. Single all her life, she poured it out for one great thing: to make Jesus Christ known among the unreached, the poor, and the sick. Laura was a widow, a medical doctor, pushing eighty years old, and serving at Ruby's side in

Cameroon. The brakes failed, the car went over a cliff, and they were both killed instantly. I asked my congregation: Was that a tragedy? Two lives, driven by one great passion, namely, to be spent in unheralded service to the perishing poor for the glory of Jesus Christ—even two decades after most of their American counterparts had retired to throw away their lives on trifles. No, that is not a tragedy. That is a glory. These lives were not wasted. And these lives were not lost. "Whoever loses his life for my sake and the gospel's will save it" (Mark 8:35).

An American Tragedy: How Not to Finish Your One Life

I will tell you what a tragedy is. I will show you how to waste your life. Consider a story from the February 1998 edition of *Reader's Digest*, which tells about a couple who "took early retirement from their jobs in the Northeast five years ago when he was 59 and she was 51. Now they live in Punta Gorda, Florida, where they cruise on their 30-foot trawler, play softball and collect shells." At first, when I read it I thought it might be a joke. A spoof on the American Dream. But it wasn't. Tragically, this was the dream: Come to the end of your life—your one and only precious, God-given life—and let the last great work of your life, before you give an account to your Creator, be this: playing softball and collecting shells. Picture them before Christ at the great day of judgment: "Look, Lord. See my shells." *That* is a tragedy. And people today are spending billions of dollars to persuade you to embrace that tragic dream. Over against that, I put my protest: Don't buy it. Don't waste your life.

Pretend I Am Your Father

As I write this, I am fifty-seven years old. As the months go by, I relate to more and more people who are young enough to be my sons and daughters. You may be in that category. I have four sons and one daughter. Few things, if any, fill me with more longing these months and years than the longing that my children not waste their lives on fatal success.

This longing transfers very easily to you, especially if you are in your twenties or thirties. I see you, as it were, like a son or a daughter, and in these pages I plead with you as a father—perhaps a father who loves you dearly, or the father you never had. Or the father who never had a vision for you like I have for you—and God has for you. Or the father who *has* a vision for you, but it's all about money and status. I look through these pages and see you as sons and daughters, and I plead with you: Desire that your life count for something great! Long for your life to have eternal significance. Want this! Don't coast through life without a passion.

I Love the Vision of Louie Giglio

One of the inspirations behind this book was my participation in the conferences for college students and young adults called Passion '97, Passion '98, Passion '99, and now OneDay. Under Christ, the spark plug behind these worship and mission-mobilizing gatherings was Louie Giglio. He is calling young people to make a "268 Declaration." The number comes from Isaiah 26:8—"Yes, LORD, walking in the way of your laws, we wait for you; your name and renown are the desire of our hearts" (NIV). The first statement of the "Declaration" says, "Because I was created by God and for His glory, I will magnify Him as I respond to His great love. My desire is to make knowing and enjoying God the passionate pursuit of my life."

This vision of life holds out to students and young adults so much more than the emptiness of mere success or the orgy of spring break. Here is not just a body, but a soul. Not just a soul, but a soul with a passion and a desire. Not just a desire for being liked or for playing softball or for collecting shells. Here is a desire for something infinitely great and beautiful and valuable and satisfying—the name and the glory of God—"your name and renown are the desire of our hearts." This is what I live to know and long to experience. This is virtually the mission statement of my life and the church I serve: "We exist to spread a passion for the supremacy of God in all things for the joy of all peoples through Jesus Christ." You don't have to say it like I say it or like Louie Giglio says it. But whatever you do, find the God-centered, Christ-exalting, Bible-saturated passion of your life, and find your way to say it and live for it and die for it. And you will make a difference that lasts. You will not waste your life.

The Man Whose Single Passion Made All Else Rubbish

You will be like the apostle Paul, as we saw earlier, when he said that he wanted to know nothing but Jesus Christ and him crucified. Nobody had a more single-minded vision for his life than Paul did. He could say it in many different ways. He could say: "I do not account my life of any value nor as precious to myself, if only I may finish my course and the ministry that I received from the Lord Jesus, to testify to the gospel of the grace of God" (Acts 20:24). One thing mattered: "I will not waste my life! I will finish my course and finish it well. I will display the Gospel of the grace of God in all I do. I will run my race to the end."

Or he could say, "Whatever gain I had, I counted as loss for the sake of Christ. Indeed, I count everything as loss because of the surpassing worth of knowing Christ Jesus my Lord. For his sake I have suffered the loss of all things and count them as rubbish, in order that I may gain Christ" (Phil. 3:7–8). One thing matters: Know Christ, and gain Christ. Everything is rubbish in comparison to this.

What is the one passion of your life that makes everything else look like rubbish in comparison? Oh, that God would help me waken in you a single passion for a single great reality that would unleash you, and set you free from small dreams, and send you, for the glory of Christ, into all the spheres of secular life and to all the peoples of the earth.

Christ Crucified: The Blazing Center of the Glory of God

Life is wasted if we do not grasp the glory of the cross, cherish it for the treasure that it is, and cleave to it as the highest price of every pleasure and the deepest comfort in every pain. What was once foolishness to us—a crucified God—must become our wisdom and our power and our only boast in this world.

God created us to live for his glory, and that God is most

glorified in us when we are most satisfied in him. We magnify God's worth the most when *he* becomes our only boast. His glory can only be seen and savored by sinners through the glory of Jesus Christ. Any other approach to God is illusion or incineration. If we would make much of God, we must make much of Christ. His bloody death is the blazing center of the glory of God. If God is to be our boast, what he did and what he is in Christ must be our boast.

The Shocking Summons to Boast in a Lynching Rope

In this regard, few verses in the Bible are more radical and sweeping and Christ-exalting than Galatians 6:14: "Far be it from me to boast except in the cross of our Lord Jesus Christ, by which the world has been crucified to me, and I to the world." Or to state it positively: Only boast in the cross of Jesus Christ. This is a single idea. A single goal for life. A single passion. Only boast in the cross. The word "boast" can be translated "exult in" or "rejoice in." Only exult in the cross of Christ. Only rejoice in the cross of Christ. Paul says, Let this be your single passion, your single boast and joy and exultation. *May the one thing that you cherish, the one thing that you rejoice in and exult over, be the cross of Jesus Christ.*

For Paul to say that we should boast only in the cross of Christ is shocking for two reasons. One is that it's like saying: Boast only in the electric chair. Only exult in the gas chamber. Only rejoice in the lethal injection. Let your one boast and one joy and one exultation in the lynching rope. "May it never be that I would boast, except in the cross of our Lord Jesus Christ." No manner of execution that has ever been devised was more cruel and agonizing than to be nailed to a cross and hung up to die like a piece of meat. It was horrible. You would not have been able to watch it— not without screaming and pulling at your hair and tearing your clothes. You probably would have vomited. Let this, Paul says, be the one passion of your life. That is one thing that is shocking about his words.

The other is that he says this is to be the *only* boast of your life. The only joy. The only exultation. "Far be it from me to boast except in the cross of our Lord Jesus Christ, by which the world has been crucified to me, and I to the world." What does he mean by this? Can he be serious? No other boast? No other exultation? No other joy except the cross of Jesus?

What about the places where Paul himself uses the same word to talk about boasting or exulting in other things? For example, Romans 5:2: "We *rejoice* in hope of the glory of God." Romans 5:3–4: "More than that, we *rejoice* in our sufferings, knowing that suffering produces endurance, and endurance produces character, and character produces hope." Second Corinthians 12:9: "I will *boast* all the more gladly of my weaknesses, so that the power of Christ may rest upon me." First Thessalonians 2:19: "What is our hope or joy or crown of *boasting* before our Lord Jesus at his coming? Is it not you?"

"Boast Only in This" Means "Let All Boasting Be Boasting in This"

So, if Paul can boast and exult and rejoice in all these things, what does Paul mean—that he would not "boast except in the cross of our Lord Jesus Christ"? Is that just double-talk? You exult in one thing, but say that you are exulting in another thing? No. There is a very profound reason for saying that all exultation, all rejoicing, all boasting in anything should be a rejoicing in the cross of Jesus Christ.

Paul means something that will change every part of your life. He means that, for the Christian, all other boasting should also be a boasting in the cross. All exultation in anything else should be exultation in the cross. If you exult in the hope of glory, you should be exulting in the cross of Christ. If you exult in tribulation because tribulation works hope, you should be exulting in the cross of Christ. If you exult in your weaknesses, or in the people of God, you should be exulting in the cross of Christ.

Christ Bought Every Good Thing and Every Bad Thing That Turned for Good

Why is this the case? Because for redeemed sinners, every good thing—indeed every bad thing that God turns for good—was obtained for us by the cross of Christ. Apart from the death of Christ, sinners get nothing but judgment. Apart from the cross of Christ, there is only condemnation. Therefore everything that you enjoy in Christ—as a Christian, as a person who trusts Christ—is owing to the death of Christ. And all your rejoicing in all things should therefore be a rejoicing in the cross where all your blessings were purchased for you at the cost of the death of the Son of God, Jesus Christ.

One of the reasons we are not as Christ-centered and

cross-saturated as we should be is that we have not realized that everything—everything good, and everything bad that God turns for the good of his redeemed children—was purchased by the death of Christ for us. We simply take life and breath and health and friends and everything for granted. We think it is ours by right. But the fact is that it is not ours by right. We are doubly undeserving of it.

1. We are *creatures*, and our Creator is not bound or obligated to give us anything—not life or health or anything. He gives, he takes, and he does us no injustice (Job 1:21).

2. And besides being creatures with no claim on our Creator, we are *sinners*. We have fallen short of his glory (Rom. 3:23). We have ignored him and disobeyed him and failed to love him and trust him. The wrath of his justice is kindled against us. All we deserve from him is judgment (Rom. 3:19). Therefore every breath we take, every time our heart beats, every day that the sun rises, every moment we see with our eyes or hear with our ears or speak with our mouths or walk with our legs is, for now, a free and undeserved gift to sinners who deserve only judgment.

Welcomed Mercy or Mounting Wrath?

I say "for now" because if you refuse to see God in his gifts, they will turn out not to be gifts but High Court evidence of ingratitude. The Bible speaks of them first as "the riches of his kindness and forbearance and patience" that point us to repentance (Rom. 2:4). But when we presume upon them and do not cherish God's grace in them, "Because of your hard and impenitent heart you are storing up wrath for yourself on the day of wrath when God's righteous judgment will be revealed" (Rom. 2:5).

But for those who see the merciful hand of God in every breath they take and give credit where it is due, Jesus Christ will be seen and savored as the great Purchaser of every undeserved breath. Every heartbeat will be received as a gift from his hand.

Deserving Nothing but Inheriting Everything— Why?

How then did he purchase them? Answer: By his blood. If I deserve nothing but condemnation because of my sin, but instead get life and breath in this age, and everlasting joy in the age to come, because Christ died for me, then everything good—and everything bad that God turns for good—must be the reward of his suffering (not my merit). This includes all that diversity that I wondered about at the beginning of this message. I asked, can work and leisure and relationships and eating and lovemaking and minis-try all really flow from a single passion? Is there something deep enough and big enough and strong enough to hold all that together? Can sex and cars and work and war and changing diapers and doing taxes really have a God-exalt-ing, soul-satisfying unity? Now we see that every experi-ence in life is designed to magnify the cross of Christ. Or to say it another way, every good thing in life (or bad thing graciously turned for good) is meant to magnify Christ and him crucified.

Did Christ Buy My Totaled Dodge?

So, for example, we totaled our old Dodge Spirit a few years ago, but nobody was hurt. And in that safety I exult. I glory in that. But why was nobody hurt? That was a gift to me and my family that none of us deserves. And it won't always be that way. But this time it was, and we didn't deserve it. We are sinners and by nature children of wrath, apart from Christ. So how did we come to have such a gift for our good? Answer: Christ died for our sins on the cross and took away the wrath of God from us and secured for us, even though we don't deserve it, God's omnipotent grace that works everything together for our good. So when I exult in our safety, I am exulting in the cross of Christ.

Then the insurance paid us for the car, and my wife Noël took that money and went to Iowa and bought a Chevy Lumina that was one year newer and drove it home in the snow. And I exult in the amazing grace of so much bounty. Just like that. You wreck your car. You come out unhurt. Insurance pays up. You get another one. And you move on almost as if nothing had happened. And in thanks I bow my head and exult in the untold mercies even of these little material things. Where do all these mercies come from? If you are a saved sinner, a believer in Jesus, they come through the cross. Apart from the cross, there is only judgment—patience and mercy for a season, but then, if spurned, all that mercy only serves to intensify judgment. Therefore every good thing in life, and every bad thing that God turns for good, is a blood-bought gift. And all boasting—all exultation—should be boasting in the cross.

Woe to me if I exult in any blessing of any kind at any time, unless my exulting is an exulting in the cross of Christ.

Another way to say this is that the design of the cross is the glory of Christ. The aim of God in the cross is that Christ would be honored. When Paul says in Galatians 6:14, "Far be it from me to boast except in the cross of our Lord Jesus Christ," he is saying that God's will is that the cross always be magnified—that Christ crucified always be our boast and exultation and joy and praise—that Christ gets glory and thanks and honor for every good thing in our lives and every bad thing that God turns for good.

Spreading a Passion for Christ Crucified—By Teaching

But now here's a question: If that is the aim of God in the death of Christ—namely, that "Christ crucified" be honored and glorified for all things—then *how* is Christ to get the glory he deserves? The answer is that this generation has to be taught that these things are so. Or to say it another way: The source of exultation in the cross of Christ is education about the cross of Christ.

That's my job. I am not alone, but I do embrace it for myself with a passion. This is what I believe the Lord called me to in 1966 when I lay sick with mononucleosis in the health center in Wheaton, Illinois. This is where it was all leading—God's mandate: So live and so study and so serve and so preach and so write that Jesus Christ, the crucified and risen God, be the only boast of this generation. And if this is my job, yours is the same, just in a different form: to live and speak in such a way that the worth of

"Christ crucified" is seen and savored by more and more people. It will be costly for us. It was costly for him.

The Only Place to Boast in the Cross Is On the Cross

If we desire that there be no boasting except in the cross, then we must live near the cross—indeed we must live on the cross. This is shocking. But this is what Galatians 6:14 says: "Far be it from me to boast except in the cross of our Lord Jesus Christ, *by which the world has been crucified to me, and I to the world.*" Boasting *in* the cross happens when you are *on* the cross. Is that not what Paul says? "The world has been crucified to me, and I [have been crucified] to the world." The world is dead to me, and I am dead to the world. Why? Because I have been crucified. We learn to boast in the cross and exult in the cross when we are on the cross. And until our selves are crucified there, our boast will be in ourselves.

But what does this mean? When did this happen? When were we crucified? The Bible gives the answer in Galatians 2:20: "I have been crucified with Christ. It is no longer I who live, but Christ who lives in me. And the life I now live in the flesh I live by faith in the Son of God, who loved me and gave himself for me." When Christ died, we died. The glorious meaning of the death of Christ is that when he died, all those who are his died in him. The death that he died for us all becomes our death when we are united to Christ by faith (Rom. 6:5).

But you say, "Aren't I alive? I feel alive." Well, here is a need for education. We must learn what happened to us. We must be taught these things. That is why Galatians

2:20 and Galatians 6:14 are in the Bible. God is teaching us what happened to us, so that we can know ourselves, and know his way of working with us, and exult in him and in his Son and in the cross as we ought.

Linking with the Death and Life of Christ Crucified

Consider Galatians 2:19–20 again. We will see that, yes, we are dead and, yes, we are alive. "I have been crucified with Christ [so I am dead]. It is no longer I who live, but Christ who lives in me. And the life I now live in the flesh [so, yes, I am alive, but it isn't the same "I" as the "I" who died] I live by faith in the Son of God, who loved me and gave himself for me." In other words, the "I" who lives is the new "I" of faith. The new creation lives. The believer lives. The old self died on the cross with Jesus.

You may ask, "What's the key for linking up with this reality? How can this be mine? How can I be among the dead who are alive with Christ and who see and savor and spread the glory of the cross?" The answer is implied in the words about *faith* in Galatians 2:20. "The life I now live . . . I live by *faith* in the Son of God." That is the link. God links you to his Son by faith. And when he does, there is a union with the Son of God so that his death becomes your death and his life becomes your life.

Dying, Living, and Boasting in the Cross

Now let's take all that over to Galatians 6:14, and we will see how we come to live totally for the glory of Christ crucified. "Far be it from me to boast except in the cross of our Lord Jesus Christ, by which the world has been crucified to me, and I to the world." That is, don't boast in anything except in the cross. How shall we become so radically cross-exalting? How can we become the kind of people who trace all our joy back to joy in Christ and him crucified? Answer: The old self that loves to boast and exult and rejoice in other things died. By faith we are united to Christ. His death becomes the death of our self-exalting life. We are raised with him to newness of life. What lives is a new creature whose single passion is to exalt Christ and his cross.

To put it another way, when you put your trust in Christ, your bondage to the world and its overpowering lure is broken. You are a corpse to the world, and the world is a corpse to you. Or to put it positively, according to verse 15, you are a "new creation." The old "you" is dead. A new "you" is alive. And the new you is the you of faith. And what faith does is boast *not* in the world, but in Christ, especially Christ crucified.

This is how you become so cross-centered that you say with Paul, "I will not boast, except in the cross of our Lord Jesus Christ." The world is no longer our treasure. It's not the source of our life or our satisfaction or our joy. Christ is.

Shall We Prize What He Presents or What It Portrays of Him?

But what about safety in the car accident? What about the insurance payment we received? Didn't I say I was happy about that? Isn't that worldly? So am I really dead to the world? Dead to insurance payments and new cars?

I pray that I am dead in the right way. I believe that I am.

Not perfectly, I am sure, but in a real sense. How can this be? If I feel glad about safety or health or any good thing, and if these things are things of the world (which they are), then am I dead to the world? Yes, because being dead to the world does not mean having no feelings about the world (see 1 John 2:15; 1 Tim. 4:3). It means that every legitimate pleasure in the world becomes a blood-bought evidence of Christ's love, and an occasion of boasting in the cross. We are dead to insurance payments when the money is not what satisfies, but Christ crucified, the Giver, satisfies.

C.S. Lewis illustrates what I mean by an experience he had in a toolshed.

> I was standing today in the dark toolshed. The sun was shining outside and through the crack at the top of the door there came a sunbeam. From where I stood that beam of light, with the specks of dust floating in it, was the most striking thing in the place. Everything else was almost pitch-black. I was seeing the beam, not seeing things by it.
>
> Then I moved, so that the beam fell on my eyes. Instantly the whole previous picture vanished. I saw no toolshed, and (above all) no beam. Instead I saw, framed in the irregular cranny at the top of the door, green leaves moving on the branches of a tree outside and beyond that, ninety-odd million miles away, the sun. Looking along the beam, and looking at the beam are very different experiences.[1]

The sunbeams of blessing in our lives are bright in and of themselves. They also give light to the ground where we walk. But there is a higher purpose for these blessings. God means for us to do more than stand outside them and admire them for what they are. Even more, he means for us to walk into them and see the sun from which they come. If the beams are beautiful, the sun is even more beautiful. God's aim is not that we merely admire his gifts, but, even more, his glory.

We Die to the Innocent World in the Blaze of Christ's Glory

Now the point is that the glory of Christ, manifest especially in his death and resurrection, is the glory above and behind every blessing we enjoy. He purchased everything that is good for us. His glory is where the quest of our affections must end. Everything else is a pointer—a parable of this beauty. When our hearts run back up along the beam of blessing to the source in the blazing glory of the cross, then the worldliness of the blessing is dead, and Christ crucified is everything.

The Only God-Glorifying Life

This is no different than the goal of magnifying the glory of God. Christ is the glory of God. His blood-soaked cross is the blazing center of that glory. By it he bought for us every blessing—temporal and eternal. And we don't deserve any blessings. He bought them all. Because of Christ's cross, God's elect are destined to be sons of God. Because of his cross, the wrath of God is taken away. Because of his cross all guilt is removed, and sins are forgiven, and perfect righteousness is imputed to us, and the love of God is poured out in our hearts by the Spirit, and we are being conformed to the image of Christ.

Therefore every enjoyment in this life and the next that is not idolatry is a tribute to the infinite value of the cross of Christ—the burning center of the glory of God. And thus a cross-centered, cross-exalting, cross-saturated life is a God-glorifying life—the *only* God-glorifying life. All others are wasted.

GETTING TO THE BOTTOM OF YOUR JOY

[This chapter is a lightly edited transcript of what was originally preached on January 3, 2011 at Passion 2011 in Atlanta, Georgia. Audio of this message is available online at http://dsr.gd/passioncon2011.]

Several times I have asked a particular question at these Passion conferences. Let me give you the question and then tell you where we're headed with it in this message.

The question is, *Do you feel more loved by God when he makes much of you, or do you feel more loved by God when He frees you and enables you, at great cost to His Son's life, to enjoy making much of Him forever?*

Let me shorten it down so you can hear the essence of it. *Do you feel more loved by God because he makes much of you, or because he enables you to make much of him?*

Clearing Up a Misunderstanding

I've asked the question numerous times around the country, and what I have come to realize is that it has led to some significant misunderstandings that I hope to clear up here. So this message is designed to bring clarity and precision to that question: what I mean by it, and what it doesn't mean.

Let me say it again. *Do you feel more loved by God because he makes much of you or because he, through Christ, enables you to enjoy making much of him forever?*

I think I have misled. For example, I think some people respond and say, "So Piper really doesn't believe that God makes much of us, or if he does, he doesn't think we should be happy about it or joyful in it because if we are happy that God makes much of us, then that contaminates our happiness in making much of him. That seems to be what Piper thinks."

That's not what I think. I don't want to mislead you. I don't want you to be left with unbiblical or disproportionate thoughts about these things. I want clarity. I want to be faithful to the Bible. What I'm after is biblical clarity and precision about what God is saying to us is. It really doesn't matter in the end what I think. It matters what God thinks, and the only way we know what God thinks is because he has revealed himself to us, and has revealed what he thinks about a lot of things, in the Bible. And so all I care about, and all you should care about, is what does God think about this question I've been asking. What is God's answer to that question, or what should your answer be in God's eyes? I don't deny—indeed, I affirm with all my might—that God makes much of those who are in Christ. And we will come back to that shortly, and you will find things in the Bible that simply are beyond your imagination concerning how he makes much of you.

Why Ask Such a Question?

So what am I trying to do with that question? If it's risky to ask a question like this one, which is open to misunderstanding, why would I use it? Why would I go around forcing this issue? *Do you feel more loved by God because he makes much of you or because he enables you to make much of him?*

I do it because I'm trying to help people. I'm trying to help you in this message exchange what's at the very bottom of your joy. I want you to exchange self at the bottom of your joy with God at the bottom of your joy. That's what I'm after in asking that question.

Let me clarify what I mean by "the bottom of your joy." I have a picture in my mind, and I hope you can keep it in yours in this message. All of our joys have a foundation, except one. Any happiness that you have in something has a foundation, except one. The one that has no foundation is the bottom.

What's at the Bottom?

I'll give you an example. You make an A on a test, and it makes you very happy. That's understandable. I think that's a good thing. And somebody asks you, *Why are you happy about making an A on a test*? There could be many different answers. You can say, "It'll make mom and dad happy," or "I love the praise of my teachers," or, "It's going to be key in getting into graduate school in psychology." But then what if someone asks you, "Will just getting into graduate school make you happy?" And you might say, "Perhaps, because I've always had the dream of being a clinical psychologist, and I can't be one unless I go to graduate school in psychology. That's why the A leading to the graduate school makes me happy because then I can be what I've dreamed about being."

But then go deeper. Why do you want to be a clinical psychologist? Why does that make you happy? Why is this such a feeder for happiness? You might say, because you would love to help people, or it makes you happy to think about the possibility of helping people by knowing them and giving God's perspective on how their mind works and their emotions work and their relationships work—that would make you happy.

So now, we're down about four levels. And then I would ask, Why does helping people make you happy? Now, we're getting close to the bottom, aren't we? And the bottom is where there aren't any more answers. When you get to the bottom, you might say, "You just do." It's who you are. Where you end up as you penetrate down in your life to the bottom of what makes you happy is who you are. And there are two possibilities down there: making much of you or making much of God. And my hope in this message is to be used by the Holy Spirit to remove making much of self from the bottom and replace it with making much of God. Or you could simplify it as: self versus God.

Only you and God know your heart and how it's working right now and what makes you happy. There are so many layers of happiness, and they all have foundations. But one foundation has no foundation. And is that one foundation God or self? That's what my question is designed to illuminate.

Different Worlds; Different Destinies

So let me ask it again. Do you feel more loved by God—or we could say, do you feel happier—because God makes much of you, or because God enables you to enjoy making much of him? I am not denying that God makes much of you, but I am forcing a ranking. I'm asking about the order at the bottom. When you get down to the bottom of your life, there is a ranking—either self is first, or God is first. I'm not denying that God makes much of us. It's a glorious thing to be enabled by the atoning blood of Jesus and the Holy Spirit to be freed from self and make much of God as your supreme joy and life, and it's a glorious thing to delight in being made much of by God. But everything hangs on their ordering, their ranking, their placement at the bottom or not. That's what I'm after in this question. *Do you enjoy worshiping God, making much of God, because at the bottom, this God that you're worshiping is committed to making much of you?* That's idolatry of the worst kind.

Or do you enjoy God's making much of you because it shows you the kind of God that He is? His making much of us enables us and equips us and transforms us so that we can actually see him for who he is, and love him for who he is, and treasure him for he is, and be satisfied in him for who he is. That's the bottom. Those are different people, different worlds, different destinies; that's what I'm after in that question. I want to hit people in the face with the deepest issue of their lives, and that takes a miracle to change. That miracle is called the new birth.

What It Means to Be Born Again

Why does this matter so much to me? Why is getting to the bottom of our joys such a big deal to me? I believe that there are perhaps millions of professing Christians who are not born again who believe God loves them and yet who are bound for hell, confident that they are loved by God and feeling it. That's why I ask that question; that's why it matters to me. Hundreds of you in this room perhaps feel loved by God but you're not born again, because what you mean by being loved by God is that, at the bottom, he's committed to making much of you. He's not at the bottom, you're at the bottom and you don't want that. You don't want it short term, and you don't want it long term. Millions of nominal Christians have never experienced the fundamental alteration in the foundation of that happiness.

The most fundamental thing that happens in the new birth is an exchange from myself as the source of all my joys, and myself being made much of, to God being the source of all my joys, and him being the bottom. Jesus becomes the supreme treasure. To know him and to make much of him becomes my deepest joy feeding all my other joys. In other words, all my fountains are in him. He has become the bottom. All my other desires, if I'm walking in him, are rising up out of that spring. He is the fountain from which all the other desires are coming. If there's any holiness in getting an A, it is because of him at the bottom.

I ask the question because it seems to me millions of nominal Christians are not born again. They haven't experienced this. Test yourself as I describe what is so tragically and fearfully true about so many. They have interpreted conversion to Jesus to mean that they can have all the same deepest desires they had before they were converted, only now the desires are met by another person, Jesus. So to get converted, for example, would mean that always if you always wanted to be wealthy and I've always sought it in the wrong places, now in Jesus there's a way to have what you've always wanted. Jesus is the way. He gives me what I always wanted: money. That's not new birth. You can sing to him till doomsday, jumping up and down, and it will not be anything pleasing to him.

Or you might have always wanted to be healthy. Now, instead of going to all the doctors, you go to Jesus. "Did we not do many mighty works in your name?" some will one day ask Jesus. "Did we not cast out demons in your name? Did we not prophecy in your name? Did we not heal in your name?" And Jesus will say to them, "I never knew you. Depart from me workers of iniquity." That might be the scariest verse in the Bible! Miracles, prophecy, exorcism in Jesus's name, and they are hell-bound. Do you think this is not an important question to ask?

What's at the bottom? So many professing Christians are on their way to destruction. Many of us would agree that wealth and health can be problems, but what if what you've always wanted is not to go to hell? And now, you hear one day, that there's a way not to suffer forever. His name is Jesus. "Yes, I don't want hell," you say, "so I'll take Jesus—since he's the way out of hell."

But what's at the bottom? Pain-free skin. No eternal suffering. But that's not the new birth. The new birth is not loving the same meal, but having a different butler. It's not having the same suitcases in your hotel room full of the same stuff, but with a different bellhop. That's not the new birth. The new birth is something new at the bottom. The suitcases at the bottom are different; the meal at the bottom is different.

Helping You Have God at the Bottom

To become a Christian, in this way of seeing things (this way that I'm describing here) is to have all the same desires you have before you were born again, but now you just get them from a new place—and when you get them, you feel loved by God. That's very dangerous. So I'm asking, *Do you feel more loved by God if he makes much of you in all these ways, or have you experienced such a revolution in your heart that what is your deepest joy in your life is making much of God?* That's why I ask the question. The new birth changes the bottom, the root, the foundation of what makes us happy. Self at the bottom is replaced with Jesus at the bottom. This is why it matters to me so much. So I'm trying to help you put God at the bottom with his beauty and his value as your one deepest desire, feeding all your other desires. God is the fountain, the spring that explains everything you're happy about in life.

I'm not denying that God makes much of you. I want to affirm that with all my mind—and that's where we're headed. I want you to feel loved by God, but I'm so jealous that you not feel loved by God when he is not at the bottom.

So then, let's ask this: *Why in the Bible does God perform all of his acts of love to us in such a way that the design of those acts of love is manifestly to make much of himself?*

God's Design in Making Much of Us

Let me say that again. As I read my Bible, from beginning to end, and try to zero in on the places where it's really clear that God loves us, I'm amazed to discover what else God has to say in that context about why he's doing such acts of love. Does it terminate on me or on him? Does his loving me signify that I'm at the bottom, and that he's making my worth the foundation of everything, or is he doing it in such a way that it puts him at the bottom and makes his work the foundation of everything? My answer is that he always makes much of us in such a way as to make himself the bottom.

So I would like to give just a few examples this because you may not be familiar with the Bible enough to say, "Why can't I think of some text where that is true?" So let me illustrate what I mean when I say that throughout the Bible God loves us in such a way as to make clear that his design in loving us is that he would be made much of. His design in making much of us is to make clear that his goal is that he'd be made much of.

God Shows His Love for Us by Adopting Us

First, Ephesians 1:5–6:

> In love he predestined us for adoption as sons
> through Jesus Christ, according to the purpose of
> his will, to the praise of his glorious grace ...

God predestined us for adoption into his family. This happened before you were born. This is amazing love. And then there's this phrase: "to the praise of the glory of God's grace."

Why is God loving you into his family? Answer: So that you would spend your eternity making much of his grace. So there it is—this is the kind of thing I mean. It's all over the Bible—love towards me with the view toward making much of God. Whether you are wired to feel loved by is crucial to who you are. There are professing Christians all over the world who would hear that and say, "I don't feel loved when you talk like that." Watch out.

So I'm asking, "Why does God talk like that?" He knows that some people are going to say, "I'm not feeling loved when you tell me that you're making much of me so that you get made much of. I'm not feeling loved by that." Why does he talk like this? I'll give you another text to illustrate.

God Shows His Love for Us by Sending Us a Savior

Second, Luke 2:10–14:

> "Fear not, for behold, I bring you good news of
> great joy that will be for all the people. For unto
> you is born this day in the city of David a Savior,
> who is Christ the Lord. And this will be a sign for
> you: you will find a baby wrapped in swaddling
> cloths and lying in a manger." And suddenly there
> was with the angel a multitude of the heavenly
> host praising God and saying, "Glory to God in
> the highest, and on earth peace among those with
> whom he is pleased!"

Now, that is really something. A Savior has been born for sinners like me, and sinners like you. A Savior is born! I'm being loved on Christmas. I'm being pursued by God on Christmas. My sins will be forgiven, my guilt will be taken away, my condemnation will be renewed. God loves me and is after me.

So what do the angels say? *You are awesomely worthwhile.* That's not what they say. That's what we say if you're born again. We say, "Glory to God in the highest! I've been saved!" That's the way you talk when you're born again. You don't say, "What a good boy am I, or, I'm a diamond in the rough—he bought me, you know. He's a good investor." You don't talk like that—not if you're born again. It's sad that there are Christians who talk like that. They say things like, "The cross is evidence of how valuable I am." But we should turn that right on its head—the cross is a manifestation of the unspeakable grace of God. We will spend eternity making much of God because he saved us.

So I'm loved *for his sake.* And when you're born again, that's the way you want it to be. The regenerate wouldn't have it any other way. They don't want to be at the bottom. They want his glory at the bottom—that's what it means to be born again.

There are far too many people who are all into God because they think God has made them the bottom.

God Shows His love for Us in the Death of Jesus

Third, 2 Corinthians 5:14–15:

> The love of Christ controls us, because we have concluded this: that one has died for all, therefore

all have died; and he died for all, that those who
live might no longer live for themselves but for him
who for their sake died and was raised.

Was it for our sake? Yes. Was it for his glory? Yes. And
everything hangs on *how* you get that right.

Are you glad to be died for, to be loved by the blood of
Jesus, by the suffering Savior? Yes, we are. And why? This is
what Paul says: "He died for all, that those who live might
no longer live for themselves." I think that he means essentially "might no longer live with themselves at the bottom,
needing to be made much of as the bottom and the source
of all the joys, but rather now live for him who, for their
sakes, died and was raised."

So the bottom of our joy is the glory of Christ in making much of Christ.

At one of the first Passion conferences in 1998, the title of
my message was "Did Christ Die for Us or for God?"[2] The
answer to that question was, "Yes, He did die for us, but he
died for us with a specific design that he manifests clearly
in the Bible—that we would make much of him." That's his
deepest goal—that's what's at the bottom and is ultimate.

God Shows His Love for Us in the Way Jesus Prays for Us

Fourth is John 17, the longest prayer of Jesus in the Bible.
You should feel greatly loved by this prayer. He's praying
for you. He says in verse 20, "I do not ask for these only,
but also for those who will believe in me through their
word." And he's praying for us today as he did then. We
should feel greatly loved. Jesus is praying for you, he's

interceding for you, he's on your side. But listen to what he says in verse 24:

> Father, I desire that they also, whom you have given me, may be with me where I am, to see my glory that you have given me because you loved me before the foundation of the world.

So, what is he praying for me? He says, "Father, I love those who are in me by faith—those whom you have given me. And I'm asking this for them. My supreme request is that you cause them to be with me that they may see how glorious I am." That's what he's praying for you.

So, we ask, "Is this prayer for me or for him?" The born-again person is happy to say, "It's for me because it's for him. He is at the bottom and I'm resting on him. He's loving me, interceding for me, and drawing me to himself because he is supremely valuable, and to see him and know him and enjoy him and show him is my greatest joy."

To be born again is to experience that—to hear John 17:24 and to say, "Yes!" Heaven isn't endless golf or endless virgins or endless health, but it's endless Jesus, seeing him, loving him, treasuring him, having him at the bottom as my greatest joy.

Why Does God Do It This Way?

The reason I point to those four texts is simply to show you the tip of the iceberg that runs throughout the Bible. I could give you dozens more texts. They are all over the Scriptures. Throughout the Bible when God shows us his love for us, the surrounding contexts again and again show that he loves us with the specific design that he be made much of *in* and *through* and *because of* that act of love.

Now we ask, Why does he do it this way when he knows that some people will feel unloved when they hear that he is loving us so that he gets the glory?

Remember, I'm trying to answer and clarify the question, *Do you feel more loved by God because he makes much of you, or because he enables you to make much of him?* Before I give you the answer to why God talks like this, I am going to do what I've never done at Passion and give you seven ways that God makes so much of you.

How God Makes Much of Us

What follows is just Bible, and it's absolutely mindboggling. I ask the Holy Spirit to come in the next few minutes as you read through these texts and give you supernatural capacities to feel the truth and the wonder of what God says here, to the praise of Jesus's name. God makes much of all those who are in Jesus. *God makes much of you,* if you believe in Jesus, if you trust him, and he's your treasure and the bottom of your joy.

So, how does he make much of us who believe?

1) God makes much of us by being pleased with us and commending our lives.

One of C.S. Lewis' greatest sermons was called "The Weight of Glory." Reading it changed my life in 1968. There C.S. Lewis describes what he believes is the weight of glory that every Christian will gloriously bear: the words "Well done, good and faithful servant."

> To please God . . . to be a real ingredient in the
> divine happiness . . . to be loved by God, not merely
> pitied, but delighted in as an artist delights in his
> work or a father in a son—it seems impossible, a
> weight or burden of glory which our thoughts can
> hardly sustain. But so it is.[3]

I think Lewis is right.

Imagine you, a sinner, receiving this kind of commendation—from God. Some of you labor under the emotional burden that all you do is just displease God. Your shortcomings are everywhere. You don't read the Bible the way you should, or pray the way you should, or talk the way you should, or witness the way you should. You come to the end of everyday feeling hopeless.

Can you imagine that because of Christ, and your connection to him by faith, the Holy Spirit moves in your life, causes you to be born again, puts Jesus at the bottom, and God commits himself to say to you one day, "Well done, good and faithful servant"? God will say that to the thief on the cross who turned to Jesus. I don't think there's a select number of Christians that hear, "Well done!" while the rest hear, "Lousy life. You basically blew it all the time, but you can come in anyway." I don't think anyone will hear that out of the mouth of Jesus at the last day. The thief on the cross who lived more than 99.9 percent of his life as a pagan and only half an hour as a born-again believer and heard from Jesus, "Today, you will be with me in paradise"— this same converted thief will hear Jesus say, "Well done!"

God makes much of us by being pleased with us through Jesus Christ.

2) God makes much of us by making us fellow heirs with his Son who owns everything.

God makes much of us by making us fellow heirs, an inheritor with his son who inherits everything in the universe. Here are some texts:

> Matthew 5:5: "Blessed are the meek, for they shall inherit the earth." Not just Atlanta, Georgia, or the United States, but all the planet, the whole earth.

> Romans 4:13: "The promise to Abraham and his offspring [is] that he would be heir of the world."

> 1 Corinthians 3:21–23: "Let no one boast in men. For all things are yours, whether Paul or Apollos or Cephas or the world or life or death or the present or the future—all are yours, and you are Christ's, and Christ is God's." Francis Chan could probably illustrate this better than I. Perhaps he would set up some scales and put those statements on one side. "You Christian will inherit everything, everything. This is why I pray that you have the capacity to believe." He would say, "You live like that—it's out of sync. The scale is falling off the table. My life is not reflecting the kind of freedom from grumbling that you have when you're two seconds away from inheriting billions and billions of dollars, namely, the universe."

John Newton, who wrote "Amazing Grace," told this little parable about a man who was on his way to a big city to inherit a million dollars—which would be a whole lot more money today, let's just say $100 million. You're on your way to inherit $100 million, and you're riding in a horse-drawn carriage (we'll leave the carriage and not update that to a car) on your way happily to inherit $100 million. You're not far away from the city when a wheel falls off your carriage.

Here's a picture of our lives. We're not that far from home. This life is called a vapor's breath—like just two seconds. We'll call the broken carriage suffering, our light and momentary affliction. We're that close to our inheritance, we really are. Some reading this message will die this year; others, maybe in 70 years. But they're both virtually the same, and make little difference in light of eternity. It's that close, and then forever.

But Newton says that instead of running the rest of the way to get his inheritance, the man who has the broken wheel stumbles all the way into the city, grumbling the whole way, "My chariot is broken, my chariot is broken." That's a picture of our lives. I see myself in that mirror, and I hate it. That's what Francis Chan meant when he said that our lives should be in accord with the gospel. The gospel has this in it. God makes much of us by granting us to inherit the world, and it's that far away—so why would you need to have it now?

Oh, Jesus makes much of you. Yes, He does.

3) God makes much of us by having us sit at the table when Jesus returns, and he serves us as though he were a slave and we were the masters.

Did you know that the Bible says that? I'll read it to you. It's from a parable in Luke 12:37:

> "Blessed are those servants whom the master finds awake when he comes. Truly, I say to you, he will dress himself for service and have them recline at table, and he will come and serve them."

Not only is this what happened on the night before Jesus died, but also it will surely happen when he comes again, riding on a white horse, with a sword coming out of his mouth, as King of kings, Lord of lords, with "faithful" written on one thigh and "true" on the other, the mighty God himself (Rev. 19:11–16). And once he sits on the throne and divides the nations, he comes down and finds himself with the towel and tells us, "Children, sit, sit," and he serves us.

Yes, you are made much of, and you will be made much of breathtakingly in that day.

4) God makes much of us by appointing us to carry out the judgment of angels.

How many angels are there? At least one hundred million. It says in Daniel 7:10 that "ten thousand times ten thousand stood before him." It may be lots more, but it's at least one hundred million.

When the apostle Paul is talking to this rag-tag ordinary group of disciples at Corinth, who can't figure out how to settle their own disputes, his argument for why they should be able to judge right and wrong, and settle their own disputes, is that one day they will be qualified to judge angels.

> When one of you has a grievance against another, does he dare go to law before the unrighteous

instead of the saints? 2 Or do you not know that
the saints will judge the world? And if the world
is to be judged by you, are you incompetent to
try trivial cases? 3 Do you not know that we are
to judge angels? How much more, then, matters
pertaining to this life! (1 Corinthians 6:1–3)

However ordinary you may think you are, Paul would
look into your face and say that one day you will judge
angels. Now, I don't know what that involves. I just know
this: it's not a small thing. He's not making little of you
when he says that.

5) God makes much of us by ascribing value to us and rejoicing over us as His treasured possession.

Matthew 10:31:

"Fear not, therefore; you are of more value than
many sparrows."

Zephaniah 3:17:

The Lord your God is in your midst,
    a mighty one who will save;
he will rejoice over you with gladness;
    he will quiet you by his love;
he will exult over you with loud singing.

If I hear that correctly, what he's saying is that in the last
day, when God is done working on you, you will not simply be pleasing to God—you will be thrilling to God. I
don't ever feel thrilling to God. I regularly feel like a failure in my sanctification. So I need all the help I can get

from the Holy Spirit to believe Zephaniah 3:17, that one day, the love that God has for me now will come to a consummation in having so worked in me that he will look upon me and be thrilled. Here's another, Matthew 13:43:

> "The righteous will shine like the sun in the
> kingdom of their Father."

I love that text. I've tried every now and then to look at the sun, and I can't. It will blind you if you look at the sun. So this text says, God's children, his people, one day will shine like the sun—which means nobody will be able to look at you with natural eyes. This is why C.S. Lewis says that one day people will be tempted to bow down and worship you, except that they will all be made perfectly holy, and they'll know better. But you will look like you're worthy of it because you will shine like the sun.

6) God makes much of you by granting you to sit with Jesus on his throne.

This is perhaps the most amazing one. This is Revelation 3:21, and Jesus is talking:

> "The one who conquers, I will grant him to sit with
> me on my throne, as I also conquered and sat down
> with my Father on his throne."

That's scary. It sounds almost heretical. Is he going to put us on the throne of God? No, we won't go on the throne of God. Here's what I think it means, and God help me because I'm sure I don't get it all.

Paul says in Ephesians 1:23 that the church is "his body,

the fullness of him who fills all in all." The universe is going to be filled with Jesus, and I think that probably means his manifest rule will extend, with no competitors, to the end of creation. And Ephesians 1:23 says that we are that fullness. I think this means something like sitting on the throne—that is, Jesus's rule will be exercised through us. He will share the rule of the universe with the likes of us.

Yes, God Makes Much of Us—But Why?

So let it be said loud and clear now, as I close, that I do not deny, and never have denied, that God makes much of us. The question is ranking. Whether these amazing truths that ought to thrill our soul—and, yes, they should—are the very bottom of our joy or not. God makes much of us, and it should thrill our souls. But why? And if the answer is because you're at the bottom, and you love to be made much of, that's no evidence of being born again.

But if your answer is that God making much of me reveals more of God to me, and equips me to know him more, treasure him more, love him more, be satisfied in him more, then that is good evidence of being born again. That's the difference between the regenerate and the unregenerate: what's at the bottom.

A Love That's Even Greater

Let's go back to the question I said I would try to answer. *Why does God all over the Bible reveal his acts of love toward us in a way that shows his design is that he get glory?* The answer is this: God's love for you, a love that makes much of his glory, is a greater love for you than if he made you your greatest treasure. God's love for you, a love that makes him your supreme treasure, is a greater love for you than if he made you your supreme treasure.

Why? Because self, no matter how glorious—and it one day will be glorious—can never satisfy a heart made for God. It feels so good to the fallen heart. It feels so good to have myself at the bottom and to be made much of. And until we're born again, we can't realize that self won't satisfy us. We will never be beautiful enough, strong enough, wise enough, admirable enough to be the bottom of our joy, and bear the weight of all the joy that you want for eternity. Self will not bear that weight. It will give way, and you will fall into the pit.

Only one thing can bear the weight of all the joy that you ache for forever: God.

God loves you. I want you to feel loved, and God wants you to feel loved. You are precious to him. You are *precious* to him. And the gift the gift that he would want me to give you at the close of this message is to say this: "I love you, and you are so precious to me that I will not let your preciousness become your God. I will be your God. And I alone."

JOY AS THE POWER TO SUFFER IN THE PATH OF LOVE FOR THE SAKE OF LIBERATION

[This chapter is a lightly edited transcript of a message preached on January 3, 2013 at Passion 2013 in Atlanta, Georgia. Audio and video are available online at http://dsr. gd/passioncon2013.]

The apostle John lifted up his eyes to heaven and God granted him to see a glimpse of why the universe exists. And he wrote it down so that we could know. He wrote:

> I saw in the right hand of him who was seated on
> the throne a scroll written within and on the back,
> sealed with seven seals. ² And I saw a mighty angel
> proclaiming with a loud voice, "Who is worthy to
> open the scroll and break its seals?" ³ And no one
> in heaven or on earth or under the earth was able
> to open the scroll or to look into it, ⁴ and I began
> to weep loudly because no one was found worthy

to open the scroll or to look into it. [5] And one of the elders said to me, "Weep no more; behold, the Lion of the tribe of Judah, the Root of David, has conquered, so that he can open the scroll and its seven seals."

[6] And between the throne and the four living creatures and among the elders I saw a Lamb standing, as though it had been slain, with seven horns and with seven eyes, which are the seven spirits of God sent out into all the earth. [7] And he went and took the scroll from the right hand of him who was seated on the throne. [8] And when he had taken the scroll, the four living creatures and the twenty-four elders fell down before the Lamb, each holding a harp, and golden bowls full of incense, which are the prayers of the saints.

[9] And they sang a new song, saying, "Worthy are you to take the scroll and to open its seals, for you were slain, and by your blood you ransomed people for God from every tribe and language and people and nation, [10] and you have made them a kingdom and priests to our God, and they shall reign on the earth."

[11] Then I looked, and I heard around the throne and the living creatures and the elders the voice of many angels, numbering myriads of myriads and thousands of thousands, [12] saying with a loud voice, "Worthy is the Lamb who was slain, to receive power and wealth and wisdom and might and honor and glory and blessing!"

¹³ And I heard every creature in heaven and on earth and under the earth and in the sea, and all that is in them, saying, "To him who sits on the throne and to the Lamb be blessing and honor and glory and might forever and ever!" ¹⁴ And the four living creatures said, "Amen!" and the elders fell down and worshiped.

There are several things that are crystal clear from Revelation 5. Here are a few of them.

First, Jesus is the key that unlocks the mystery of history. And when the key unlocks the mystery of history and the story is told, he turns out to be the main reality in the story. So he unlocks the mystery of history, and he is the center of the story of history.

Second, John tells us that the reason that Jesus is worthy to open the mystery of history is that he was a lamb who was slain and a lion who conquered. It was the purpose of God that the center of the story of the universe be a lion-like lamb and a lamb-like lion.

Third, the achievement of Jesus when he triumphed, being slain as a lamb, purchased people for God from every tribe and tongue and people and nation and made them kings and queens to God, and turned them into priests to spend eternity praising the Lord Jesus.

Fourth, the upshot of this achievement is that Jesus is infinitely worthy of eternal admiration from every creature in heaven, on the earth, under the earth, and in the sea, because of His infinite glory. "Worthy is the Lamb who was slain, to receive power and wealth and wisdom and might and honor and glory and blessing!" (Rev. 5:12).

He's worthy of everlasting honor and praise and admiration. Here's another way to say it: the universe exists to display the infinite worth of Jesus in the white-hot worship of millions of angels, and all the creatures, and millions of the ransomed from every people group on the earth.

In other words, our worship is the subjective echo of God's objective worth. The immensity of his worth is reflected in the intensity of your worship. We were made for the admiration of the excellence of Jesus, and the greater your admiration, the greater the revelation of Christ's glorification. You see the connection between the intensity of your admiration and the display and the clarity of his excellence and his glorification in the world.

The Pleasure of Admiration

It is a great irony to me that the atheist, novelist, philosopher Ayn Rand spoke it so plainly and truly when she said, "Admiration is the rarest and the highest of pleasures." And she didn't know why; she didn't know the ultimate reason why God made her that way. The reason admiration is in fact the greatest pleasure of the human soul is that God made the world and fashioned the human soul so that Jesus would be glorified, and we would be satisfied, in the very same act of the soul, namely, glad-hearted admiration of the excellence of Jesus. We are satisfied in the intensity of our enjoyment of Him, and He is magnified and glorified in our being satisfied in Him. That's the way God made the universe and that's why admiration is so rare—and why it is the greatest pleasure that the soul was made to experience.

Which means that in this universe the intensity of our joy in the greatness of Jesus is a demonstration of the immensity of his beauty and worth. Or as we love to say, *Jesus is most glorified in us when we are most satisfied in Him.* The universe exists for the glorification of Jesus in the admiration of his people. It exists to display the infinite worth of the lamb in the white-hot worship of his people.

And lest that is too ethereal for you to get a handle on, let's say a little more from the Book of Revelation about this future.

Unhindered Joy in God Forever

In the endless ages of eternity there will be no obstacle to the greatness of our joy in the greatness of God. There are many obstacles now. Right now most of you are encountering huge obstacles to the kind of joy that Jesus deserves from you. Daily, we meet daily huge emotional, circumstantial, and satanic obstacles. In the age to come there will be none—no death, no sickness, no pain, no crying, no calamity, and best of all, no sin in here, no sin out there.

And not only will there be no obstacles to the fullness and the intensity of your joy in Jesus, but there will be a perfect abundance of new creative outlets for the expression of our joy—new name; new crown; new food from the Tree of Life; new song; new heaven with the glory of God replacing the sun and the moon; new earth, where lion and lamb lie down together, and the wolf and the lamb graze together; new city, where every cultural good that makes people love cities will be there and all the misery and all the sin that makes people hate cities will not be there. There will be no obstacle to your joy and abundance. Instead there will be a perfect abundance of new creative outlets for the experience of your joy in God. If you are in Christ—that's a big if—if you are in Christ, if you are trusting Christ, that's your future. That's where you are going, that's your reward: an everlasting life of joy expressed in ten thousand ways, your admiration of the infinite worth of Jesus, with no hindrance coming from inside you, no hindrance coming from outside you, just maximum joy in the beauty of Christ, an eternal citizenship in a new city, a new paradise with no obstacles and only endless outlets for your joy in the greatness of Jesus.

Embracing Suffering

Now what I've been doing for the last ten minutes, is laying a foundation for your ability to embrace suffering in the path of love in the cause of liberation. That's what I've been doing. And when I say *liberation*, I mean liberation from the whole scope of Satan's wicked kingdom and thralldom that holds so many people in so many different kinds of bondage.

If you follow the path of love in the cause of liberation from the darkness of the devil in whatever form, you will suffer. And the aim of this message is to put this foundation under your feet and show you from the Bible how this foundation empowers you not just to endure, but to embrace suffering in the path of love until you're dead. That's where we're going.

So I'm referring to every form of liberation from Satan's thralldom: liberation for the slaves of the multibillion dollar sex industry, or the sweat shops of greed, or the armies of cruelty where boy soldiers are forced to practice killing on their parents. That includes the liberation of 125,000 children that every day are cut to pieces in their mother's wombs, in every country of the world including our so-called civilized America, including this squeaky clean city of Atlanta where yesterday probably one out of every four pregnancies ended in abortion.

I care about that slavery; the slavery of the abortionists and the slavery of those being lied to about what they have inside them, the slavery of those who populate your campuses by the thousands and who face an eternal fate ten thousand times worse than any slavery on this planet, the slavery of the people you walk among every day. I'm talking about every level of slavery sending you to embrace suffering in the path of love, in the cause of liberation.

If you follow that path you will suffer, and I don't say that because I'm a prophet, I say it because the Bible says it, over and over again:

> 2 Timothy 3:12, "All who desire to live a godly life in Christ Jesus will be persecuted."

> Matthew 10:25, "If they have called the master of the house Beelzebul, how much more will they malign those of his household."

> John 15:20, "If they persecuted me, they will also persecute you."

> 1 Peter 4:12, "Do not be surprised at the fiery trial when it comes upon you to test you, as though something strange were happening to you."

> 1 Thessalonians 3:3, "That no one be moved by these afflictions. For you yourselves know that we are destined for this."

> Psalm 34:19, "Many are the afflictions of the righteous."

> Romans 8:23, "We who have the firstfruits of the Spirit, groan inwardly as we wait eagerly for adoption as sons, the redemption of our bodies."

> John 16:2, "The hour is coming when whoever kills you will think he is offering service to God."

If you follow Jesus in the path of love you will suffer. So here's what we're going to spend the rest of our time doing: We're going to go to look at a few verses from the Book of Hebrews chapters ten, eleven, and twelve. I hope for the rest of your life you will be able to say: "I saw a pattern of power to suffer in Hebrews that I had never seen before, and it has served me well in my life of sacrifice ever since Passion 2013. That's my goal.

The Biblical Pattern of Embracing Suffering

Let me give you the pattern; I'll just describe it and then we're going to go see it in the Bible. What I think doesn't matter. What this Bible says matters infinitely. But let me just describe where we're going in three steps and we're going to go to those three passages and see these three steps in every one of them.

1. This is the pattern of power to embrace suffering in the path of love for the cause of liberation; that's what this is. A heart, your heart joyfully treasuring the

promised reward that I just spent fifteen minutes trying to describe—a paradise, a new paradise, a new city, a new crown, a new freedom from sin, and best of all, seeing Christ face to face and expressing in ten thousand fresh ways your admiration of Him. A deep, present satisfaction in that future glorious hope; that's number one, first layer.

2. That soul satisfaction in your Christ-saturated future frees you from self-protecting fear.

3. That freedom from self-protecting, self-enhancing, and self-gratifying fear releases you to embrace suffering in the cause of love for others. Those are the three steps.

Now that is what I want you to see in the Bible, and it is amazing. These passages in Hebrews have simply stunned me for years, and I want so bad at age 66 to still learn this and be this.

The Pattern in Early Christians

So let's go to Hebrews 10:32–35. "Recall the former days when, after you were enlightened"—that is, brought into the light of Christ, saved, born again—"you endured a hard struggle with sufferings, sometimes being publicly exposed to reproach and affliction, and sometimes being partners with those so treated. For you had compassion on those in prison [or you could say, slavery], and you joyfully accepted the plundering of your property, since you knew that you yourselves had a better possession and an abiding one. Therefore do not throw away your confidence, which has a great reward."

Verse 34 describes some Christians. Some are in prison for their faith. Some are not in prison for their faith. And those who are not in prison are facing a choice: will we go to the prison and align ourselves with the ones who are in prison and thus risk our lives and our homes and our property and our children? Will we risk it, or will we play it safe and not care about those who are now in prison? That's the choice they had to make, and something *not amazing* happened when they went to the prison and something *utterly amazing* happened when they went to the prison. What happened that was *not amazing* is that they were persecuted and their property was plundered. And what happened that *was amazing* is that they rejoiced in the plundering of their property. This is verse 34: "you had compassion on those in prison, and you *joyfully accepted the plundering of your property.*" That's the 60,000 I want to send out.

When your room is trashed and they write graffiti on your wall about Christians, and roll their eyes, and lock you in, and put you out, I want you to be so rooted in the first fifteen minutes of this message that you can rejoice in that. That would be an absolute miracle. That would be a miracle, and that's the miracle Louie is after. That's the miracle I'm after; that's what Passion is about—the glorification of the infinite worth of Jesus so that he stays our joy when everything around our soul gives way.

The question is, how did they do that? And the answer is crystal clear. It goes like this: "You joyfully accepted the plundering of your property, since you knew you yourselves had a better possession and abiding one." They had a city. They had a paradise. They had a sinless future on the way. They had an abundance of outlets for everlasting infinite joy coming their way, and it had broken into their lives with such amazing conviction that they did not need to grumble or worry or fret or be angry, or resentful, or bitter about their persecution. They rejoiced and sang all the way to the prison. That's Hebrews ten, and it is utterly amazing.

Their foundation was laid in that they had a reward that was better, infinitely better. "You make known to me the path of life; in your presence there is fullness of joy; at your right hand are pleasures forevermore" (Ps. 16:11). Nothing the world can offer or take can compare with that, and therefore, I'm free from my self-protecting fear. I'm on my way to the prison and the slave camps, and I will love out of this hope.

The Pattern in Moses

Now let's go to Hebrews 11:24–26. This is the same pattern. "By faith Moses, when he was grown up, refused to be called the son of Pharaoh's daughter, choosing rather to be mistreated with the people of God than to enjoy the fleeting pleasures of sin. He considered the reproach of Christ greater wealth than the treasures of Egypt, for he was looking to the reward." That's exactly the same amazing argument and pattern.

You may be wondering, why have you used the word *embrace* suffering so often and not just *endure* suffering? Why do you keep talking about we need to *embrace* suffering? My answer is verse 25: Moses "*choosing* to be mistreated with the people of God rather than to enjoy the fleeting pleasures of sin." It didn't sneak up on him, and then he had to endure it unexpectedly; he looked it square in the face. It was walking right at him. And he walked right into it, and embraced it for the next forty years of his life. He chose to love his people at huge cost. He could have stayed in Egypt with every possible worldly pleasure for as long as he lived and he said, "I'm leaving it, and I'm walking with this people who are going to grieve me over and over again, because I look to the reward and these are fleeting and that's not."

So there's the pattern. Moses's soul satisfaction was in the Messiah-saturated future, released from self-protecting fear to give himself to the reproaches of a people in the name of the Messiah. And thus, he set the slaves free from Egypt in that hope and that satisfaction and walked away from earthly pleasure.

The Pattern in Jesus

Chapter twelve is perhaps the most amazing one, the most controversial one, and the most important one. Hebrews 12:1–2: "Therefore, since we are surrounded by so great a cloud of witnesses, let us also lay aside every weight, and sin which clings so closely, and let us run with endurance the race that is set before us, looking to Jesus, the founder and perfecter of our faith, who for the joy that was set before him endured the cross, despising the shame, and is seated at the right hand of the throne of God." Now that's the greatest act of liberation that has ever happened in the history of the world. The Son of God suffered the agony and the infamy of the cross in order to bear our sins and deliver us out of the slavery of death and hell and sin. Revelation 1:5: "To him who loves us and has freed us from our sins by his blood"—the greatest act of freeing, of liberation, happened when Jesus died in our place and bore our sins and paid our debt.

And the question is: how did the God-man have the wherewithal to embrace the cross and endure the cross? Where did it come from? It says in verse two, "For the joy that was set before Him He endured the cross." This is exactly the same pattern as Moses, and the early Christians. His infinitely holy, sinless heart was steadied and satisfied by the joy of knowing what He was about to achieve. "No one takes it from me, but I lay it down of my own accord. I have authority to lay it down, and I have authority to take it up again" (John 10:18). He's walking into this suffering with his eyes wide open and he says, "What is steadying me, what is strengthening me, what is holding me, is the joy that is set before me of my triumph over sin and Satan and hell and death and my gathering an untold number of ransomed who will spend eternity with me, enjoying me, and worshiping me; that prospect strengthens me and gets me through; the same principle as the one that drives you if you get this and live in it."

So let me sum it up.

> The early Christians joyfully embraced suffering—the suffering of liberation—because they had a better possession and an abiding one.

> Moses embraced the suffering of liberation because he saw the pleasures of Egypt as fleeting and he looked to the reward.

> Jesus embraced the suffering of liberation because he was sustained by the joy that was set before him.

Motivated By Reward?

Forty years ago I was studying in Germany and my topic was Jesus's command to love our enemies and the motivation that would sustain loving enemies. I was reading widely in ethical literature, and it seems like everywhere I turned the standard teaching was this: If you do a good deed for a reward, you have destroyed its goodness. And the argument was that if you do good for somebody *for your reward* you're not loving, you're selfish. It was a watershed moment for me, a kind of test. And it came down to this: You ethical teachers, you're telling me, you're provoking me, you're tempting me to be motivated in my acts of love by a higher motivation than my Savior? That's blasphemy. Will I follow you, or will I follow what I see in these texts? Jesus looked to the reward, a better possession and an abiding one, for the joy that was set before him. I am driven. Which way will I go? Follow my worldly wisdom that seems so right and is so dead wrong? Or will I go with the Bible? We all have these watershed moments in our lives; this may be one of them for you right now.

All the satisfaction that the early Christians had, and that Moses had, and that Jesus had, as they looked to the reward, was the power not to be selfish but to be free from selfishness. It freed them from the self-protection of fear. It released them. This focus on our glorious Christ-filled, all-satisfying future, freed them for love. It didn't make them selfish; it broke the power of selfishness in their lives so that they laid their lives down for people over and over again.

And if you ask, and you should, why isn't it selfish to

love a person for your own reward? That's a good question, and here's the answer: It is not selfish to love another person for your reward in Jesus because that reward, and your satisfaction in it, is the very power that is moving you to lay down your life for them. And your goal in laying down your life for them is to include them in the very reward that is motivating you. Nobody can call that *selfish*.

Conclusion

This message began with the exaltation of the Jesus who promises us a future of a new city and a new paradise and a new crown and a new heaven and a new earth where there will be no obstacles to our joy, and an abundance of outlets for every creative bone in our bodies to manifest his worth through all the good that he has made. And then we move to say you're going to suffer if you walk in the path of love in the cause of liberation. The Bible says so, not me. And then we said there's a pattern for how to do that, and the pattern has three steps:

1. The foundation of soul satisfaction comes from the streaming into the present that glorious future with Jesus.

2. Soul satisfaction in Jesus releases you from self-protecting fear into power.

3. Loving acts of sacrifice liberate the captives.

It is no accident that the greatest chapter in the Bible— Romans 8—ends with Paul bending every truth-laden effort to sustain our all-satisfying hope because of the sufferings we will have to endure. Let his words—the very words of God—set you free from self-protecting fear in the path of love for the sake of Christ-exalting liberation.

> What then shall we say to these things? If God is for us, who can be against us? He who did not spare his own Son but gave him up for us all, how will he not also with him graciously give us all things? Who shall bring any charge against God's elect? It is God who justifies. Who is to condemn? Christ Jesus is the one who died—more than that, who was raised—who is at the right hand of God, who indeed is interceding for us. Who shall separate us from the love of Christ? Shall tribulation, or distress, or persecution, or famine, or nakedness, or danger, or sword? As it is written, "For your sake we are being killed all the day long; we are regarded as sheep to be slaughtered." No, in all these things we are more than conquerors through him who loved us. For I am sure that neither death nor life, nor angels nor rulers, nor things present nor things to come, nor powers, nor height nor depth, nor anything else in all creation, will be able to separate us from the love of God in Christ Jesus our Lord. (Rom. 8:31–39)

NOTES

1   C.S. Lewis, "Meditation in a Toolshed," in *C.S. Lewis: Essay Collection and Other Short Pieces* (London: Harper Collins, 2000), 607.

2   See http://dsr.gd/passion1998

3   C.S. Lewis, "The Weight of Glory," in *The Weight of Glory and Other Addresses* (Grand Rapids: William B. Eerdmans Publishing Company, 1965), p. 10.

❄ desiringGod

The mission of Desiring God is that people everywhere would understand and embrace the truth that God is most glorified in us when we are most satisfied in him. Our primary strategy for accomplishing this mission is through a maximally useful website that houses over thirty years of John Piper's preaching and teaching, including translations into more than 40 languages. This is all available free of charge, thanks to our generous ministry partners. If you would like to further explore the vision of Desiring God, we encourage you to visit www.desiringGod.org.

Desiring God

Post Office Box 2901, Minneapolis, Minnesota 55402
888.346.4700   mail@desiringGod.org

6780654R00061

Printed in Germany
by Amazon Distribution
GmbH, Leipzig